En

2 In 1

Strategies You Should Know About As A Sensitive Person To Enjoy Life To The Fullest

By

Joseph Salinas

Table of Contents

Empath Strategies

Introduction 10

Chapter 1: What It Means To Be An Empath 14
    Energy And Emotion 22

Chapter 2: Empaths, Emotions, And Health: How To Stop Absorbing Others' Distress 31

Chapter 3: Empaths And Addiction, From Alcoholism To Overeating 38
    Seek Help 40
    Find Other Means Of Stress Relief 40

Chapter 4: Empaths, Love, And Sex 41
    Problems With Love 42
    Communication 44
    Your Partner's Happiness Is His/Her Responsibility 46

Get To Know Someone First 47
Don't Take Things Personally 51
Be Your Own Person 51

Chapter 5: Protecting Yourself From Narcissists And Other Energy Vampires 55

Narcissists 56
Sociopaths And Psychopaths 65
Borderlines 72
Manipulators 76

Chapter 6: Empaths, Parenting, And Raising Sensitive Children 83

Patience And Understanding 83
Don't Punish Your Child For Moodiness 84
Teach Coping Skills 85
Don't Over Medicate 87
Being An Empathic Parent 88

Chapter 7: Empaths And Work 90

Enjoy Your Work 90
Avoiding Burnout In Helping Professions 93
Dealing With Co-Workers' And Clients' Energy ... 97

Chapter 8: Empaths And Society 100

Set Distance From Other People 101

Always Put Yourself First 103

Focus On The Spiritual 105

Unplug From The Electronic Universe 105

Engage In Regular Energy Cleansing 106

Value Quality More Than Quantity 107

Maintain Your Privacy 108

Have A Healing Home Space 109

Chapter 9: Empath Friendships And Relationships 111

How To Maintain A Healthy Relationship With An Empath 112

Setting Healthy Boundaries 114

Achieving Balance 116

HSPs With Non-HSPs 117

When Both Of You Are HSPs 120

Chapter 10: Challenges For Empaths 123

Odd Sleep Patterns And Insomnia 123

Adrenal Fatigue 124

Maintaining A Healthy Diet 125

Physical Health 126
Addictive Behaviors... 127
Mental Health.. 127
Discernment.. 128

Chapter 11: Empaths And Communication 130

Shy Vs. Silent.. 130
Rapid Speech And The Solution......................... 131
Rambling And The Solution............................... 132
Direct Conversation 134
One-Sided Conversation 136
Brain Chatter And The Solution 136
Power In Speech 137
Complaining And The Solution 138
Diminished Communication And The Solution ..139
I Have Something Important To Say.................. 140

Chapter 12: Empaths And Boundaries 142

What Are Boundaries.. 142
Empaths And Boundaries 143
Allowing Boundaries.. 144

Boundaries Vs. Stress..145
Steps Before Creating Boundaries 147
Action Steps To Boundaries 147
Role-Playing..148
Stand Up And Say It...149
Is Yes To Someone Else, A No To You? 150

Chapter 13: Empath Toolbox For Navigating Energy 152

Grounding Exercise..152
Empath Gifts 153
Empath As Rescuer 154
Energetic Exchange 155
Energy Drain From You And Others 156
Numbing Out And Dealing With Distractions.....157
Tools 157

Chapter 14: Forgiveness....................168

What Can You Gain By Forgiving? 168
What Does Unforgiveness Cost You? 169
Forgiveness Vs. Unforgiveness 170
Forgiveness Saved My Life 171
How To Know If You Need To Forgive 173
Forgiveness And Equilibrium 173

Forgiveness And Relationships 174
How To Forgive 175
Forgiveness Affirmation 177
How To Tell When You've Completed Forgiving 178

Conclusion 180

Resources 183

Evolving Empath

Introduction 190

The Scientific Understanding Of Being An Empath 193
- What Is Empathy?................................193
- Three Types Of Empathy 201
- What Is An Empath? 204
- Is It Genetics? 205

Why Do Empaths Feel Things More Strongly Than Others? 208
- Some Reasons For Empaths Feeling So Deeply .208
- Why Everyone Has Different Physical Tolerances 212

Are You An Empath? 221
- What Are The Characteristics Of An Empath?....221
- Different Types Of Empaths..................230
- All About Clairs 234
- How To Figure Out Which Type You Are............235

Being An Empath............................238
- Empaths, Intuition And Extraordinary Perceptions

....238
   The Gift Of Being An Empath 241
   The Dark Side Of Being An Empath 245
   Hsps (Highly Sensitive Persons) 274
   Medics, Medications And Misdiagnoses 275

Protecting Yourself 283
   Learn How To Protect Yourself As An Empath ..283
   Strategies For Handling The Challenges Of Feeling And Absorbing So Many Stimuli 284
   Recognise 301
   Resilience 304
   Reverse - *How To Recharge When You Get 'Over-Cooked'* 332

Evolving 351
   Evolving As An Empath 351
   Grow Outside Your Comfort Zone 354

Conclusion 363
References 365
Disclaimer 373

Empath Strategies

How To Overcome Any Overwhelming Situation As A Sensitive Person

By

Joseph Salinas

Introduction

You are an empath. You are sensitive to other people and their emotions; you can practically read minds; you are a healing person, or even a healer of some type, and you love taking on the problems of others. But all in all, every good aspect of being an empathic person comes with a lot of stress and energetic drain. Can you even have a joyful, peaceful life?

You really can have a good life as an empath. Many empaths have learned to cope with the darker side of empathy, and you can, too. With science-based tips and information drawn from real-life studies, you can learn to make your life happy. You simply have to learn techniques to protect your energy and overcome challenges.

As an empath myself, I used to suffer tremendously. I was prone to negative thinking and I coped with my overwhelming emotions in an unhealthy manner. On top of that, I had no energy and suffered many stress-related health problems. Forgiveness was a problem for me, and I spent far too much of my time nursing grudges against dozens of people. My life was not happy!

With the help of various resources and an energy healer, I began to learn how to reign my gift in and control it to avoid pain. I began to study how to make my life better and use my gift constructively so that I suffered less. And I learned to manage stress, set up boundaries, and conserve my energy. As a result, I became a happier person with more power, and I got over many of my stress-related health issues. Now, I want to share my discoveries with you and help you pave the way to the same joy and success I have made for myself.

When you rid yourself of the toxic side effects of being an empath, you become an astonishingly powerful person. You have the robust powers of discernment, empathy, and emotional intelligence and you don't have to work for them the way non-empaths do. But you also don't suffer from the energetic drains that these gifts can bring you. Your health will improve, your relationships will be healthier, and your outlook on life will become more positive. The world had better watch out, because once you learn to control your gift, you will be a truly amazing person indeed!

This book is backed by fastidious research and rooted in science. The tips are real and practical, having worked for many other empaths before you. Therefore, the techniques and tools you learn in these pages are actually helpful. They will certainly change your life for the better!

I promise that by the time you finish this book, you will have all of the skills necessary to lead a fulfilling life. You will be able to treat your gift as a true gift, not a curse. You will be able to put a stop to the energy drain, pain, and negativity that can plague empaths.

Instead of spending more time in misery, start reading this book now to unlock your best life. You deserve to be happy and to bless the world with your empathic abilities. Don't let another day go by without protecting yourself.

I urge you to start reading now to make your life the best that it can be. You won't be sorry that you took this step! The journey to a joyful existence starts now, with Chapter 1!

Chapter 1: What It Means To Be An Empath

Are you an empath? You probably already suspect that you are one, or you wouldn't be reading this book. But there is more to being an empath than the Internet says.

Being an "empath" is a big trend right now. But the reality of being an empathic person is not trendy. People may believe they are empaths based on Internet quizzes or vague descriptions on Pinterest posts; however, real empaths have certain abilities and side effects that distinguish them from everyone else. People may not be so quick to label themselves as empaths if they knew what truly comes along with empathic abilities.

Having the skill of emotional intelligence or an inclination to heal others does not make you an empath. Many "normal" and non-sensitive people like to view themselves in these lenses, with no idea of what truly goes into being an empath. Normal people don't transfer energy from others and don't intuitively sense things about other people.

The hallmark of an empath is the eerie, almost psychic, ability to absorb the emotions and physical sensations of other people. Being able to practice empathy so finely makes empaths extremely talented healers. However, it can also cause them immense pain, because empaths tend to absorb the negative energy and physical ailments of those around them.

Say you see someone rubbing a soft pillow. Can you practically experience the sensation on your own skin? Any normal person could empathize with the feeling if they concentrate hard, likely because they have felt a similar material before. But an empath doesn't have to work hard to capture the feeling. An empath can tell exactly what the other person is feeling without even wanting to. The feelings of others are almost like intrusions that cannot be resisted. Transferred sensations happen to empaths constantly, often confusing empaths and disrupting their own experiences of the world.

For instance, I woke up at 4 am the morning the Orlando night club shootings happened. My skin prickled and I could practically taste the fear of many people. Of course, I had no idea what had happened, I just knew I felt upset. A few hours later, I was at my favorite donut shop and I saw the news. I knew immediately that that was what had caused my night terror!

Another example is when I enter a room of people. I can immediately sense what others are thinking and feeling. No, I can't read minds, but I can tell when someone is upset or doesn't like me. I don't have to ask or analyze someone's reactions to me. I just know.

This is what being an empath is like.

When empaths walk around, they experience lots of "noise." They experience different feelings and sensations from all of the people around them. This can feel overwhelming. An empath may not know why he or she feels so bombarded with different emotions and moods, but the experience can be completely draining. Empaths will return home after a trip to Walmart feeling totally exhausted. They have to spend lots of time recovering before they feel well enough to venture outside again. This is because they absorb the energies and suffering of many people, so crowded places and public places can be bombarding.

Empaths have trouble being in places like hospitals and funeral homes. This is because they can feel the experiences of other people who are sick or grieving. The energy can be suffocating and can make them feel sad or sick for weeks after.

In relationships, empaths can read what their

partners don't tell them. They can tell when someone is lying or hiding something. In an effort to heal their partners, they often put their own best interests aside and neglect healthy boundaries. They live to please and "fix" their partners. Without being told, they can sense when their partners are unhappy and they take it upon themselves to return their partners to a more positive state. Often, empaths inadvertently attract emotional vampires, such as narcissists and sociopaths, who prey on empaths' natural ability to absorb and cherish their partners. Empaths are often taken advantage of and abused as a result.

Empaths are often creative. They are able to capture and write, draw, or paint things they have never experienced firsthand because they are able to extract the experiences from others. They can make extremely emotional music or art or literature that perfectly illustrates the feelings of invented characters.

Last but not least, empaths are able to sense things about people. It is not a psychic ability, but rather an intense sensitivity to the feelings of others. This makes them great healers, since they know exactly what their patients are suffering and they can intuitively infer things that others can't. While a non-empath counselor may have to probe at a client to find out that she was raped, an empath can just tell. With that knowledge, he or she is able to tailor the treatment to what the client really needs, even though the client has never revealed what truly happened.

Unfortunately, while empaths are drawn to healing careers, they often don't know how to actually protect themselves. This means that empaths in healing careers can become miserable, depressed, and sick. They take on the pain of their clients and experience it like their own pain. They bleed energy without healing themselves. That is one of the issues this book addresses.

In addition, since being bombarded by the energy of others and attracting emotional vampires comes with the territory of empathic abilities, empaths often suffer various health issues. They are under intense stress all of the time, which manifests in their physical bodies. Empaths often gain or lose weight for no reason, suffer from fatigue, and have trouble healing physical wounds. They may have more sick days and more mental health problems than non-empaths. Some are driven to addiction or self-harm. All of these issues are simply caused by empaths' inability to shield themselves from the negativity of the world around them. Learning shielding and setting boundaries can reduce stress and its subsequent health problems.

Empaths are often introverted and need time alone to recuperate. They thrive when they are in certain positive environments and suffer more than most people in negative environments. Many of them love animals and Nature, and they feel a sense of replenishment when they are in the woods, on the beach, or simply in a safe space alone. It is critical that empaths take time alone and do things they enjoy, as this helps them overcome the toxicity of the world that they absorb.

Western society does not value empathy highly. It places emphasis on being professional, ruthless, and tough. This is impossible for empaths, so empaths often don't fit in and feel bullied, abused, taken advantage of, and overlooked in society. It can be hard for them to make friends and find their niches in life. Other cultures, particularly Eastern cultures, value empaths more highly. Thus, Western empaths are more prone to unhappiness and mental health issues because they are essentially outcasts, while empaths in other cultures may be happier.

Furthermore, empaths often don't do well in highly competitive or logistical careers, such as corporate careers or waiting tables. This hardly means that an empath can't succeed in such a career, but they must take special care to avoid the burnout and emotional exhaustion that inhibits their success.

Energy And Emotion

Why Are Empaths The Way That They Are?

There is strikingly little scientific research into empathic ability. The science world often dismissed "Empath" as a pseudo-scientific term with no actual evidence supporting its validity. However, the abundance of people who experience empathic abilities sheds light on the fact that empathic people are real.

However, one study does shed light on the difference between empaths and other types of people. Abigail Marsh discovered differences in brain structure in people with self-reported empathic traits [1]. Marsh's test subjects had altruistically donated kidneys without any monetary reward, so their altruism is described as "care-based" [1]. Empaths tend to have an amygdala (the region of the brain associated with fear, aggression, and other emotions) that is eight percent bigger than the control group of people who had not donated kidneys [1]. Furthermore, when shown pictures of faces expressing fear, these people had much more electrical activity in their amygdala [1]. The results are clear: Empaths are empathic because of heightened emotional sensitivity within the brain.

The deviances in brain structure in psychopaths have long been documented. Marsh's findings are that empaths have brains structured entirely opposite of psychopaths [1]. In other words, empaths are "anti-psychopaths." This makes sense, since psychopaths have no capacity for empathy and empaths have an extraordinary capacity for empathy.

Another interesting aspect of Marsh's research indicates that empaths have marked humility [1]. Empaths tend to see themselves as equals to others, instead of better than others. Therefore, they are driven to act from a place of identification and relation. When they see suffering, they know what it's like and they want to help. When they are in a position to help someone, they do so because they know what it's like to need help.

Being empathetic is hardly a sign of being an empath [2]. Most human beings, with the exception of psychopaths, have the capacity for empathy. Research indicates that empathy is a built-in characteristic inherent to survival [2]. If you can tell that someone else is scared, you know that danger is approaching and you can react [2]. Empathy helps people, who are inherently social beings, protect the group and act as a group in addressing survival issues.

However, most people only experience empathy in obvious settings. This is why facial expressions are universal [3]. You see a facial expression and you can sense what someone is really feeling and respond in kind. Empaths have such a heightened sense of empathy that they can read the most fleeting of facial expressions, which makes their "intuition" so eerily accurate [4].

Facial expressions can be incredibly fleeting if a person doesn't want to display their true emotions to others [4]. Everything a person feels will trigger involuntary muscle movements and a facial expression, known as a "leaked expression" or "micro-expression" [4]. However, if a person doesn't want to display those emotions, he or she will cover them up and replace the facial expression rapidly with a politer or more socially appropriate expression, such as smiling. Their true emotions only showed for a few microseconds [4]. Empaths have overactive amygdala, however, which causes them to pay attention and take notice of even the most fleeting expressions.

But there is more to it than that. The human brain is

wired to mimic the experiences of others, for an unknown reason [2]. When female subjects were given electric shocks to the hands, a pain matrix was observed in their brain activity on a functional MRI scan [2]. Then the subjects were told that their male spouses had received the same shocks. Their brain activity reflected an almost identical pain matrix, despite the fact that the subjects had not been shocked again [2]. This suggests that humans have an innate ability to feel what other people do.

This hardly makes sense from an evolutionary perspective. After all, what good does feeling the pain of others do you for survival? There are no answers about why this happens, only theories. One current theory is that babies are hard-wired to mimic their parents, and that wiring never entirely goes away. Another theory is that the brain is wired to create compassion in the face of pain and suffering, so that humans can take care of one another.

Energy

Many people also believe that empaths act on sensations of energy. There is little scientific evidence explaining why "vibes" occur or even if they are real or imagined. However, any empath can attest that vibes are very real. Why else would I wake up when the Orlando shootings happened, despite the fact that I was hundreds of miles from Orlando?

Energy is simply a force that exerts motion or some type of work on an object. By that definition, it makes sense that humans perceive invisible energy from other humans. It is not yet understood why or how people can put out this vaguely defined energy, but they do. This energy, in turn, influences the atmosphere of a party, the feeling of a room, and the overall mood of a crowd.

This energy may be some sort of kinetic or chemical effect from emotions. It may be something that science has not yet understood. Yet Carl Jung, a psychiatrist, may have found the answer in his theory of the collective unconscious. Jung's collective unconscious refers to a network that connects all human minds, allowing you to sense what others are thinking and feeling from great distances [5]. This collective unconscious is created from our cellular similarities to each other and is founded upon survival needs. It would explain why some people have psychic abilities, why twins separated at birth experience the same things throughout life, and why mothers know when bad things happen to their children despite geographical distance and lack of contact [5].

Emotions

Emotions are critical to our health. That much science knows. Since empaths tend to absorb the emotions of others, they tend to have greater emotional impact on their health. They are more emotional people overall, experiencing feelings that are not even theirs.

For instance, a study has linked blood pressure and emotional health [6]. When subjects of the study entered a workplace stress-reduction program, they had an overall reduction in both emotional stress and blood pressure [6]. It is clear that emotions tell your brain how to respond physically. If you are stressed out, angry, or irritated, you are flooded with adrenalin and cortisol to help you respond to the perceived disaster, even if it is not so disastrous [6]. Your blood pressure goes up and your muscles reflex.

When you are sad, depressed, or on the brink of despair, you feel tired and tend to eat to comfort yourself, which in turn causes weight gain [7]. Depression has long been linked with insomnia, weight gain or loss, loss of appetite, fatigue, oversleeping, poor wound healing, more sick days, and other distressing physical symptoms [7]. Depression can also trigger anxiety, which ups your stress levels and all of the bad effects of stress.

As an empath, you are constantly experiencing what others feel. This can make it hard to manage your own emotions and enjoy emotional peace. The emotions of others can have toxic effects on your health, even if your own emotions are sound, and you can suffer from mental health issues because of the constant negative emotions you pick up from others. To enjoy more peace of mind and more joy, you must improve your emotional resilience and thus your physical health will improve.

Chapter 2: Empaths, Emotions, And Health: How To Stop Absorbing Others' Distress

As you learned in the last chapter, your capacity for empathy can be a blessing, but it can also impact you physically in a myriad of negative ways. Mitigating the negative effects of empathic ability is the key to a joyful existence as one.

The good news is that it is more than possible to stop absorbing the distress of other people! You must perform a few mental gymnastics to begin to control the emotions that you take in and the ones you let affect you.

Differentiate

When you feel something, ask yourself if the emotion is yours or someone else's [8]. This can help you filter out the emotions that you shouldn't take responsibility for.

If you are feeling something yourself, chances are the emotion feels raw and you know the cause of it. If you are feeling someone else's, the emotion may be vague and you don't know what causes it. For instance, if your friend makes you angry and you know he did, then you know that emotion is your own. But if you are plagued by a malignant sense of depression for no apparent reason, you're probably feeling someone else's energy.

Distance Yourself From The Source

Do you notice that you always feel exhausted, angry, or sad around a specific person for no apparent reason? Does your aunt's house make you feel like you're suffocating? Do hospitals get to you?

When you are near the source and you experience their emotions, excuse yourself to use the bathroom or to take a phone call. See if the emotion lessens with distance. Often, geographic distance from the source can be helpful. Try your best to get away from people who are making you feel distressed.

Don't feel that you owe it to someone to stick around. Your health is just as important as anyone else's. You should not let other people bombard you with their energy. It is perfectly OK to take some time away from the person to clear your own emotions and gain stability.

Decide That An Emotion Doesn't Serve You

When you feel someone else's emotion, you know that it doesn't serve you. It's not even your emotion! Now that you know you are feeling someone else's distress, you can rationalize the experience, instead of dwelling on it and letting it influence your own feelings.

Start by putting the emotion into an outside perspective. "That person is really feeling awful!" This isolates the emotion and separates it from your own emotional being.

Next, focus on your breathing. Breathe out through your mouth and in through your nose. Count your breaths. This exercise centers you and distracts you from the feeling flooding your awareness.

Pay Physical Attention To The Area In Question

Every emotion triggers a flood of physical energy from a certain part of the body. In the following image, you can see where emotions concentrate according to body heat mapping [9]. In a study, participants were made to feel certain ways and then their body heat was imaged. This shows that emotions have a powerful physical effect on the body. They are actually stored, and even felt, in certain parts of the body, not just the brain.

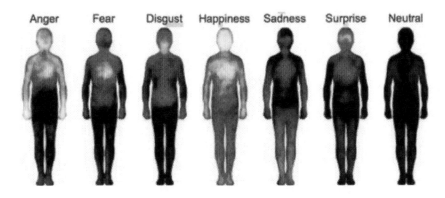

Figure 1Source 9

When you feel someone else's distress, identify the emotion in question and find the corresponding place on your body. Then place your hands over that part of your body. Imagine warmth radiating from your hands, healing this area. Think about how much you love yourself. Then imagine the feeling dissipating and this part of your body being healthy again. This will help your mind release the emotion that it has trapped in this part of your body.

Visualize Yourself Protected

Visualizations tend to work well in programming your mind to believe that something is true.

Therefore, you can train your mind to protect itself from others' emotional distress by visualizing yourself being protected.

People have different visualizations that work for them. A common one is to imagine your body sheathed in an envelope of white light that deflects all negativity. Another one is to imagine yourself wearing a coat of armor that makes you invincible to negativity. Simply visualizing yourself not feeling the emotions of others can even be helpful.

Visualize this before you go out into public or spend time around someone whom you know is negative. Do this before work and after each situation at work. You can also do this during emotional situations, such as during an encounter with an unpleasant person. Simply reflect on your visualization in your mind throughout the day to keep your mind believing that you are protected from negative emotions.

Detox

After experiencing someone else's distress, you need to spend some time in a positive environment, stat! You must clear out the negative energy and mitigate its effects on your health by making yourself happy.

After a hard day at work feeling the distress of your co-workers or clients or a particularly toxic situation such as a hospital visit, take some time to walk in nature, hike, work in a garden, do yoga, or something else that you love. Spend time around positive people, too. These things will help you cleanse yourself and feel well again.

Chapter 3: Empaths And Addiction, From Alcoholism To Overeating

Empaths are amazing people, but unfortunately, many of them are prone to addictions. Addictions can range from unhealthy addictions to food to shopping to drugs to sex. Alcoholism is often a problem empaths face. Empaths seek the pleasure of dopamine rushes from their addictions to numb out the pain that can come along with their unique abilities.

The sad fact about this is that addictions can ruin an empath's life and deaden his or her gifts. The numbness, financial ruin, potential legal troubles, and self-destruction brought on by addictions can cause more stress. Furthermore, many addictions expose empaths to the wrong people, people who don't value their gifts and prey on them. Cue destructive relationships and patterns of abuse furthered by addiction.

Many empaths are not mentally ill at all. But their gifts can create symptoms akin to mental illness, or even bring on bouts of depression and anxiety. Therefore, empaths are often heavily medicated starting at young ages. This early exposure to pharmaceutical drugs can prepare empaths for a life of addiction. While taking pharmaceutical drugs is not a life sentence to addiction, it can become that way for misguided empaths who don't learn more natural ways to cope with the pain brought on by their gifts, as empaths learn to just pop a pill for instant avoidance of their symptoms. It is essential for empaths to avoid drugs that numb or deaden their senses and alter their brain chemistry. They must also avoid self-medicating with street drugs or alcohol.

Empaths don't have to resort to harmful pastimes to relieve the stress and depression that comes along with heightened empathy. It is more than possible to relieve stress in healthy, natural ways. Read on to learn how to get over addictions and find relief in more helpful, balancing activities.

Seek Help

If you are struggling with addiction of any form, you should seek help immediately. Go to rehab or find an outpatient addiction specialist. Attend group therapy and meetings. The key to beating addiction is to stop letting it run your life.

Find Other Means Of Stress Relief

You engage in addiction in an attempt to satisfy some need within yourself. The best way to overcome addiction is to engage in some other healthier form of stress relief. For instance, do yoga instead of drinking. Put money in a savings account for a vacation instead of splurging on more clothes you don't need. Sip green tea instead of smoking marijuana. Volunteer with the homeless whenever you feel the urge to gamble.

Chapter 4: Empaths, Love, And Sex

Empaths are in a unique position to become the most loyal, attentive, and caring lovers in the world. Because they can read their partners without having to ask questions, they are more attuned to their partner's feelings and needs. They usually strive to please and fix their partners' issues. Once an empath is in love, he or she will often take on part of the partner's personality in order to bring more harmony into the relationship.

Sexually, empaths are extremely sensitive lovers. They give themselves passionately and fully. Often, they fall in love easily. Empaths should avoid the intense feelings and energetic exchanges of sex until they know a partner well. Empaths are typically not ideal candidates for casual sex. Even if they think they are, they often carry a lot of emotional baggage and energy from the other person after a sexual encounter.

Problems With Love

Sadly, empaths' dedication and loyalty can bring a few problems with it. For one, empaths tend to attract psychopaths, sociopaths, and narcissists. They want to fix these people instead of leaving them, so they tolerate mental, emotional, and even physical abuse. They allow their abusive partners to destroy their identities and dominate them completely. As they forgive every slight and wrong, they allow the abusive partner to erode their boundaries and their healthy sense of self.

Many empaths have been abused and taken advantage of the past. Thus, many of them have developed trust issues that can impede intimacy in relationships. Some of them have developed co-dependency, which makes them stick around in unhealthy relationships. Their trust issues and co-dependency are at odds, which makes them become hot and cold in relationships.

Also, empaths tend to be too sensitive. They pick up on the fact that their partners are sad, but they don't know why, so they think they are the cause of the unhappiness. They are riddled with constant energetic "noise," so they may become numb or even intolerant of additional signals from their partners. This can lead to a lot of fighting.

Empaths may become depressed because of the negative energy they absorb throughout the day, which makes them unpleasant to be around. They may have trouble gathering the energy and gusto required to be good partners to their lovers or spouses. Problems with sexual libido and intimacy created by emotional stress can cause empaths to shut their partners out unwittingly.

Some empaths deal with incredible amounts of stress. They may take this stress out on their partners. An overwhelmed empath may yell at his or her partner in the grocery store, for instance.

Many of them fear confrontation, so they avoid communicating important issues which prevents the relationship from evolving in a healthy manner. They simply work to please their partners and give into issues that they really should address. As a result, they collect pent-up unhappiness over the course of a relationship, until they finally explode in anger or withdraw completely. They basically let relationships wither and die instead of putting in the effort to improve it.

None of these issues mean that you can't be a good partner and lover as an empath. You just have to learn how to balance your gifts with the more physical and material demands of a relationship. You must also work on good communication and you must learn to avoid taking things too personally.

Communication

The single most important key for empaths to remember is that communication is key. When you have an issue, you must speak up. Holding things in is not healthy.

First, tell yourself that you are worthy. If you want your partner to change something to make you happy, then don't feel guilty. You deserve happiness. Your partner should be willing to make you happy. If he or she isn't, then you are in a bad relationship and the only solution is leaving.

Second, acknowledge that your boundaries matter. Don't worry about making someone unhappy by setting boundaries. If you need some alone time and your partner wants to hang out, make your need for alone time known. Your partner may be disappointed, but the relationship will be better in the long run. Don't let your partner's temporary happiness make you avoid setting boundaries.

Finally, realize that you can get what you want without a confrontation. Empaths naturally hate confrontation. But you can ask your partner for something without raising your voice and exchanging heated, hurtful emotions. Always speak to your partner in a calm voice. Avoid making accusations or insulting your partner. Invite collaboration with "we" terms, like "How about we talk about this?" or "I have an idea that we could use to make things better." Speak clearly about how you feel and what you want using "I" terms; for example, "I feel hurt when you are late" or "I didn't appreciate the way you just spoke to me. Can you please speak to me more gently?"

Your Partner's Happiness Is His/Her Responsibility

Empaths often mistake their natural desire to help people with the need to make people happy. Your job in this life is not to make everyone happy. You won't be able to achieve that, anyway. Someone's temporary unhappiness, and the unpleasant emotions you feel as a result are not permanent. Let them go.

Your main goal is to make yourself happy. When you do this, you can become a better lover. Take responsibility for your happiness, not your partner's. Act as a source of encouragement and support for your partner, but don't give him or her unsolicited advice or go out of your way to fix his or her every bad mood.

Don't change yourself completely to make your partner happy, either. Suggest compromises that could make both of you happy or suggest that you and your partner just aren't a good fit. You can change certain habits and behaviors to please a partner, but you should never change your core values and personality.

Get To Know Someone First

Empaths tend to get feelings quickly and jump into relationships. To avoid falling into bad relationships with energy vampires, you should take your time before sleeping with or dating someone. Always start with a casual friendship to get to know how someone really is.

Be sure to pay attention to how they treat others and how they talk about others. These are important clues as to how someone really is. A person who treats waiters poorly, gossips about her friends, and/or claims that all of his exes are terrible people who hurt him, is a person who will treat you the same way eventually. Don't let charm blind you to someone's true nature; the truth always leaks out.

Look to their past for clues, as well. It is perfectly acceptable to ask around about somebody or perform a background check. Some people might say this is paranoid behavior but doing your research on a person can prevent lots of trouble in the future. Someone with a spotty or secret past cannot be trusted; someone with a really bad reputation has earned that reputation for a reason and doesn't deserve another chance. You can probably dismiss claims about a person made by a bitter ex or old business partner, but don't dismiss continual anecdotes about how awful someone is.

Look for other signs that a person is not who he or she claims to be. For instance, if this person has lived in the same town for twenty years and has no friends, that is a good indicator that this person is not likable. If a person has a long string of exes and has gone through many divorces, chances are you'll just be another notch on the bedpost. A guy who has three kids by three different women and isn't allowed to see any of them is probably abusive in some way; a girl who keeps getting back together with her abusive ex is probably going back to him again and will hurt you. Being discerning can feel cruel because you are not giving people the second chances that you believe everyone deserves, but it's an important part of protecting yourself.

Listen to your gut. If someone makes you uncomfortable but you don't know why, take that as a sign that this person is not right for you. Never dismiss your feelings just because there is no obvious explanation for them. You are equipped with unique tools for reading people and your feelings are always spot-on, even if there is no actual evidence to validate them yet.

Also, don't let other people cloud your intuition. Maybe you don't like someone, but everyone else does. Other people convince you to give this person a chance. Then your intuition turns out to be right. You don't need to make other people hate this person, but you have every right to keep your distance. You are more sensitive than other people and you can tell things that they can't. You can't expect people to listen to you about your gut feelings, but you can take them to heart for yourself.

Don't Take Things Personally

When you sense distress in your partner, you may take it personally. Realize that your partner may have things going on that have nothing to do with you. Don't assume that his displeasure is because of you. Ask your partner why he or she is upset and listen well. Offer support and love, instead of trying to fix his or her feelings.

Be Your Own Person

To navigate relationships effectively, you must keep your own identity. Bleeding into your partner is a common problem for empaths who are in love. But this seldom bodes well for either party in the relationship. You must be your own person and avoid co-dependency to keep your relationship healthy and happy.

Be sure to establish your own life, including activities and friends that don't have anything to do with your partner. Take some time away from your partner every week to do your own things.

Get familiar with your own values. If you disagree with your partner on something value-based, don't just give in. Stand your ground and stick by your values. A good partner will never intentionally belittle or corrode your values. He or she will simply accept them.

Also, determine things that make you unhappy. These are your boundaries. For example, I don't like going to crowded events with lots of people, so that's my boundary. My wife knows not to bring me to a big party or networking event because she knows it bothers me. Instead of trying to manipulate me into going, she simply goes without me. Another boundary I have is that I don't like being lied to and I won't tolerate it. My wife is always truthful; the one time she did lie, I told her not to do it again and she apologized profusely and never did it again.

Always set your own boundaries and stand by them. When your partner violates a boundary, let him or her know. Offer consequences for when people violate your boundaries. You may not speak to someone for a while when she violates a boundary, for instance.

Finally, stop seeking validation for everything from your partner. You can and should make decisions on your own and do what you think is best. This helps separate you from your partner. While a couple needs to make huge decisions together such as whether or not to move, you will face many small decisions in your daily life that affect only you. Make these decisions on your own.

All of these things help you recharge with your own energy, so that you don't simply absorb your partner's all of the time and essentially become your partner. But if you still absorb too much of your partner's energy, you will benefit from the clearing and shielding techniques discussed in Chapter 13.

Chapter 5: Protecting Yourself From Narcissists And Other Energy Vampires

As you already know, empaths tend to draw in energy vampires. Energy vampires are people who prey on more sensitive people for their own ends. They include psychopaths, sociopaths, narcissists, borderline personality sufferers, and other malignant manipulators who see empaths as easy targets and take advantage of their natural empathy and deep caring for others.

You don't have to be a target. Learn how to identify and protect yourself from energy vampires. Always be discerning before giving someone your time and energy. Don't feel bad about shutting out people that you have categorized as "unsafe." And definitely never ignore your gut feelings about a person or situation. Your sensitivity gives you an uncanny ability to read people and predict how the future will go, but your empathy makes you tend to ignore your intuition in an attempt to forgive all people because you know that no one is perfect.

You also want to please because you hate the sensation of displeasing people, but you are not here to make everyone happy. Other people should own their emotions and not expect you to fix everything for them. You must resist the impulse to please people who are just using you. You can never make them happy; they will always want more, more, more. You should use your gifts to actually bring good to the world, not to uphold a malignant person who is using you.

Narcissists

Empaths are ideal targets for narcissistic abuse. This is because they tend to try to fix narcissists, who are often simply broken people, and they want to keep everyone around them happy to avoid the terrible energy of displeased people.

Contrary to popular belief, few narcissists are actually evil geniuses who plan how to trap and abuse innocent victims [10]. Usually, narcissists are good people at heart who just want to be loved. Empaths see that and try to help. Unfortunately, narcissists are beyond helping, unless they identify their problems and seek treatment for their personality disorder. Most narcissists are bound up in their fragile egos and live to be worshipped and loved by others, just to validate their existences [10]. They are easily hurt, so they have invented elaborate manipulative games to stave off the ego blows of being wrong, being imperfect, and being unwanted [10]. Through manipulation, they seek to control people and extort the validation they are so desperate for [10].

Narcissists are often abusive, even if they don't intend to be [10]. Empaths fall into the trap because they want to help. Many empaths operate under the false impression that with a lot of love and finesse, they can make narcissists see the errors of their ways and correct their behavior. But the truth is, you can't "make" anybody do anything. Furthermore, narcissists cannot admit that anything is wrong to them because that causes them unbelievable pain, which blinds them to the need to change and the admission that they need treatment [10].

The real way to deal with a narcissist is to refuse to play his or her games. Often, the narcissist will realize that you are not living to satisfy his or her ego, so he or she will discard you [10]. This can be painful, but you are much better off without someone with such engrained abusive tendencies in your life. Always remember that you can't fix anyone and your job is not to please a narcissist. The world won't become a better place with your gifts if you are squandering them on the bottomless ego pit of a narcissist.

Identifying And Dealing With Narcissists

You can identify a narcissist by several key behaviors.

- Never admits to wrongdoing. A narcissist must always be right, so he will never admit to wrongdoing.

He will never confess that he has any flaws. In his mind, he must be perfect and everyone must treat him as such.

- Uses gaslighting. To avoid apologizing, a narcissist will simply challenge your memory. He will tell you that you are misremembering and things didn't happen the way you said. You begin to feel insane and wonder if you have Alzheimer's because of his games.
- Needs constant attention. A narcissist will often cheat on his partner and will surround himself with a big social crowd. He needs constant ego fodder. When you can't give him all of the praise he requires, he gets it from other sources.
- Lying. A narcissist will twist the truth in any way he can in order to appear perfect. He will make himself out to be the victim and lie about his wrongdoing in any relationship. He will deny anything that challenges his superiority. He will even falsely take credit for things he did not actually accomplish.
- Grandiosity. A narcissist wants to win praise and admiration, so he will inflate himself and praise himself shamelessly. He will brag constantly about

everything he has done or everything he has. He will show things off, such as his new trophy spouse, new boat, or new watch. He makes a big show and puts on grand performances with lavish parties or loud bragging. He may make his apartment sound like the Taj Mahal when it is really crumby, or he may claim that he is a "grocery quality specialist" to make his job as a grocery store stocker sound more magnificent.

- Charm. A narcissist wants to ingratiate people and make them like him so that they feed his ego. So, he is incredibly kind, doing things for people and stroking their egos. He gives out compliments left and right. His generosity is celebrated. Everyone seems to like him.
- Deflection and defamation. When you don't do what the narcissist wants, he will punish you. He is a powerful enemy. He will make you look bad and crazy in front of others by provoking you; no one will see that he provoked you and you will look horrible for reacting. He will spread rumors about his exes. He will defame someone's character after a business deal goes sour. He will expose someone's secrets and

blackmail them.
- Using guilt. When you don't do what the narcissist wants, he is skilled at making you feel bad. He pins it all on you so you feel like a horrible person. He brings up things from the past to prove that he is right and you are wrong. By the end of his manipulation, you feel like the one in the wrong and you apologize and strive to set things right.
- Abandonment. When something no longer serves him, he walks away, with no feelings. Loyalty and history mean nothing to him. He may have walked out on his family because he was bored with them; he may quit jobs without notice because he wants better; he may simply stop talking to you and never tell you why.
- Superficiality. He is obsessed with appearances. He expects the world to be pretty for him. He is probably fastidious about his own appearance as well, or he may think that he looks really good when he doesn't.
- Uses your soft spots against you. The narcissist is great at getting to know you in a short period of time. He already knows all of your weak spots. He knows

what you want so he gives it to you to make you stick around. He also knows what hurts you and he shamelessly uses it to make you feel terrible. He does these things to manipulate you into continuing to entertain him and feed his ego.

- Invalidating your feelings and self-esteem. A narcissist will make you feel that you are wrong for feeling the way you do. He will also make you feel less than worthy of good treatment so that you never leave, assuming that no one else could want you. He may make you believe that everyone hates you or that you have some flaw. He will learn and magnify your insecurities so that you actually believe that you deserve his abuse.
- Isolating. A narcissist will isolate you so that you never leave. He will also demand so much of your time and attention that you don't have time for your own life. He may isolate you by turning you against your friends or convincing you that you are better off without them. He may act jealous when you spend time with other people so that you feel bad and stop going out. Or he may move you to an area where you

don't know anyone, so you are completely alone.
- Competition. If you went through a tough time, the narcissist has always had it worse. If you have a headache, he has a brain tumor. If you bought a house, the narcissist must assert that his house is bigger and yours really isn't anything to be proud of. The narcissist must always be the best and must always win. He will shamelessly steal the spotlight from everyone else. He will invalidate you to make you feel smaller, as well.

The best form of protection against a narcissist involves going "no contact." Simply stop talking to the narcissist. He will employ many games to make you feel guilty or he will be sweet to you to change your mind. If you continue to ignore these games, he will eventually give up and move on to his next victim.

You may also avoid playing his games if you can't go no contact. When he attempts to provoke you, just smile and refuse to react. When he tries to make himself the victim, don't say that you feel bad for him or offer to fix things. When he gaslights you, insist that your memory is perfect and then walk away instead of engaging in an argument over the past with him that you will never win. Ignoring his games will make him stop playing and move onto the next victim.

Some narcissists do care and do want to change for the better. But it's not your job to make a narcissist change for you. If he is actively seeking help in the form of therapy, support him and praise his efforts. However, don't ask him to go to therapy because he will resist and insist that there is nothing wrong.

A narcissist can be completely exhausting. Therefore, have a life away from the narcissist. Limit contact and do things you enjoy after interactions with this toxic person to clear your energy. When you feel guilty, remember that this person is mentally ill and that is not your fault or responsibility.

Sociopaths And Psychopaths

There is much debate in the psychology community about the difference between sociopaths and psychopaths. I won't go into that here because it is not important. Instead, I will lump sociopaths and psychopaths together into one category, the anti-empaths. I so named this category because both labels apply to people who totally lack the ability for empathy and who view other people as pawns, not living beings [11].

Like narcissists, anti-empaths will use you to get what they want. They will manipulate you to play their games and get the results they want. They don't do this for ego, however; they do it for results and competition [11].

Anti-empaths are not always harmful. Many of them

exist in public service positions, CEO roles, and clergy, where their unique ability to get results gives them an advantage [11]. Fifteen to twenty-five percent of violent offenders do suffer from psychopathy or sociopathy, but very few of the ones you encounter in real life are actually violent criminals or cruel abusers [11]. However, these people are still hurtful because they have no regard for you whatsoever unless you are serving them some purpose. They will happily discard you when you no longer serve them. They don't care about your emotions and don't have any ability to empathize with you. Their cold, calculating demeanors can be abrasive to empaths, who are polar opposites [1].

Identifying And Dealing With Anti-Empaths

To identify an anti-empath, look for the following traits:

- A marked lack of empathy. This person doesn't seem fazed when he sees an ASPCA ad and he laughs when people fall down. If you tell him something hurt you,

he won't appear to understand or care.
- A lack of emotion in his communication. He just doesn't acknowledge or talk about emotions at all. When someone else is expressing emotion to him, he is clueless as to how to comfort the person.
- Lack of regard for human rights. An anti-empath may not harm you if you are serving a purpose for him. But if you are not, he doesn't care at all about your rights. He doesn't care if he hurts you, or if he violates your rights, and he won't apologize. He won't let morals and ethics stop him from doing what he wants.
- Flagrant dismissal of the law. Anti-empaths often feel that they are above the law. They will happily break a law if it gets them what they want. They may even draw pride from breaking laws and rules. Even ignoring minor social rules, such as how to dress, can bring them great pleasure.
- Charm. This person is adept at making people like him. He is ingratiating, glib, and even funny. He may perform favors or offer compliments in a calculated attempt to make people want to serve his needs.

- Mood swings. This person is the nicest person on earth at one moment. The next, he is irate that things aren't going his way. He takes his emotions out on others without appearing to feel bad about it. He never apologizes for inflicting his moods upon you.
- Poor impulse control. An anti-empath will act upon impulse without regard for the consequences. Basically, he does whatever he wants in the moment. This can result in poor decision-making.
- Secrecy. You know nothing about this person's personal life or past. While some degree of impersonality is normal in work relationships, most people at least allude to some element of their personal lives once or twice. Someone who does not is likely hiding something.
- Easily bored. This person is always looking for the next stimulation or entertainment. He often treats others as a source of amusement or stimulation, without appearing to care for anyone. He swiftly abandons relationships, hobbies, jobs, and other interests without any apparent reason.
- Lack of guilt. This person can do something terrible

and laugh about it. He jokes about how he fired a whole staff or how he made a child cry. He brags about hurting others like it's a badge of honor.

- Ruthless competitiveness. This person will stop at nothing to win. When he loses, he becomes vindictive. He drives results and plans everything in advance, and really hates having his plans thwarted. He must be the best. Telling him no will certainly invoke his rage.

- Callousness. When he sees something on the news about a flood in Bangladesh, he shrugs and says, "Population control." He is coldly unfeeling and seems to regard other people as objects or even nuisances. He is not bothered by suffering or mistreatment of his fellow humans. He may be racist, bigoted, or cruel toward children and animals. He won't say that a baby is cute; instead, he will complain about how the baby's diaper stinks. Death doesn't make him sad or upset, though he does know how to fake emotions if he must. For instance, he might cry at his mother's funeral because that's what is expected of him, but he seems relatively unaffected

by the loss and continues to go through his life like normal after the funeral.
- Inability for introspection. If you ask an anti-empath to think about what he did, he won't be able to, he will shrug and say, "So I did it. What's the problem?" Reflecting on how he may have done something wrong is impossible for him.
- Extroverted. Anti-empaths cannot be alone. They constantly require attention from others for their entertainment. They are often very busy and social in order to receive the stimulation they need and find new people to use as pawns.

While the best way to deal with an anti-empath is completely avoiding him or her, this is not always possible. You may find yourself working with one, or you may have one in your family. While you should limit your time around this person, there are a few other things you can do to prevent harm.

Most anti-empaths don't have the ability to respect

people just because. You must earn respect in their eyes. Sticking up for yourself and setting clear boundaries that you stand firmly by will help you get this respect. Many anti-empaths will test your boundaries, but as long as you consistently say no, they can't get to you.

Nevertheless, some will go to any means necessary to get what they want. If you say no, they will find some way to threaten you, force you, or manipulate you into doing what they want anyway. Figure out if you can somehow strike a deal with this person to get what you want while giving them what they want. Empathize with their lack of empathy and understand that harming you does not bother them. To deal with an anti-empath, you must be cold and calculating yourself.

Don't ever rely on this person for emotional validation. The ability escapes him. He can't comfort you when you're upset, nor does he see any reason to.

If he hurts you, don't expect him to feel bad. Just tell him that he can't do something hurtful again or you will leave. He may shape up in order to keep getting things from you.

When dealing with anti-empaths, it is often helpful to show them what they will gain by doing things for you. View everything with anti-empaths as a transaction. You must offer him some type of value in order for him to do what you want. If you don't want him lying to you, point out how honesty will make you more inclined to work with him and do him favors. If you want him to nominate you for a promotion, point out the favors you will do him or the way you can recognize him from your new position. Leave out your needs or emotions, as he won't care about them at all.

Borderlines

Like narcissists suffer from narcissistic personality disorder, borderlines suffer from borderline personality disorder. These are also hurt and sick people who tend to suck the energy out of empaths, often unintentionally. While they don't usually mean harm, their unhealthy obsession with validation and their terror of abandonment can make them abusive [12]. Empaths sense their immense suffering and strive to help them at their own expense. They can quickly play into the co-dependency of borderlines, creating a very unhealthy and taxing relationship that neither party can escape.

Identifying And Dealing With Borderlines

Borderlines display the following characteristics:

- Taking things way too personally. Borderlines are terrified of being left, so they constantly demand validation that someone cares for them. They will take things far too personally and blow small slights out of proportion, taking the slightest rejection to mean that you no longer love them.
- Fear of abandonment. A borderline will do anything to keep you from leaving. He may resort to threats or

invalidating you. He may lie to cover up behavior that could drive you away.
- Clinginess. A borderline will not give you space. He or she needs your constant attention and reassurance. You may deal with meltdowns and jealous accusations if you leave for any period of time.
- Constant need for validation. A borderline will constantly ask you if you still love him, or if you like her sweater, or if you are going to make good on a promise you made. The borderline will never entirely trust you, so you may feel hurt at his or her sharp lack of trust. You must offer constant reassurance and put lots of work into keeping the borderline secure.
- Self-harm. Borderlines represent the largest group of suicide victims [12]. A borderline may use threats of self-harm to make you feel guilty so that you never leave. He may also hurt himself without thinking of the emotional harm it causes you. He may engage in reckless behavior or have addictions.
- Emptiness. A borderline will often feel empty. Nothing truly fills the void within him so he seeks thrills, love, and addictions to help him experience

something.
- Disassociation. A borderline may have times where he is not fully present in reality. Instead, he appears lost in space or daydreams. Sometimes, he says things that make no sense because he has disassociated and is not processing reality. He may briefly believe that he is someone else or located somewhere else. He may become confused when he returns to reality. In these moments, it is hard to get through to him. He may express a curious lack of emotion in a traumatizing or exciting moment because he has disassociated, as well.
- Lack of identity. A borderline has no real sense of self. He can't separate himself from other people so he doesn't have boundaries or clear rules. He may say he loves tuna one day, and the next he hates it. He may take different sides in political arguments from day to day. His moods fluctuate dramatically and you never know what to expect.

To protect yourself from a borderline, you must set very clear boundaries. Don't let this person infringe on your space. You need your own life and your own identity. You are not here to fix the borderline's issues and live for his happiness. It is acceptable to ignore his phone calls when you ask him to not call you, or to go out with friends even though she is jealous of them.

Offer the borderline lots of reassurance and love. This is what you are good at. A borderline can make for a very loyal and sweet lover if you nurture him or her. However, consider that your needs are important too. A borderline can erode your boundaries and demand so much of your attention that you have none left for yourself. Always place yourself first before caring for your partner. The borderline needs to seek help and learn to make himself happy, instead of expecting you to do it for him. A borderline who refuses to get help or work on his issues is not a safe person to be with.

When a borderline attempts to emotionally blackmail you with self-harm, just call the police. Don't show up at the borderline's house and try to save him, as that is what he wants. Put distance or leave the person altogether when he uses suicide as a form of extortion or manipulation. Anyone who uses emotional blackmail is harmful and should be avoided at all costs.

Manipulators

Some people have learned that manipulation is a surefire way to get what they want [13]. Often, these people were raised in homes where their needs were neglected, so they learned manipulation works more efficiently than direct communication. Now manipulation is a habit that they use in all areas of life.

While you may feel compassion for these people, you must not let that fuel a desire to give in to their manipulation. Manipulators are causing harm and they should not be allowed to take advantage of your innate urge to please others. Stop playing into the games manipulators attempt to rope you into.

Identifying And Dealing With Manipulators

Like narcissists, manipulators love to help. They do this to make you feel indebted them, however, as opposed to trying to feed their egos like narcissists. When a person you barely know suddenly attempts to help you generously, be very wary about accepting the help. Nothing in this life comes for free and seldom does anything come from true care-based altruism.

Manipulators are also incredibly friendly and charming. They are like this to get you to warm up to them and let them into your life. If you feel that you can tell a complete stranger anything or want to call someone you barely know a friend, take a while to really get to know the person first. See how they talk about others. Watch them interact with other people. Notice if they have patterns of gossiping, mistreating people, or leaving friendships and relationships in catastrophic ruin. A person with a bad track record is best avoided.

Also, watch out for people who play the victim and invoke your sympathy. Any person who is always the victim is probably a manipulator who fails to take responsibility for his or her mistakes in a relationship. A person who claims all of his exes abused him and cheated on him is most likely leaving out a huge part of the story; a person who seems to be having the hardest time of her life – and has been struggling with the same things for years – is likely the real culprit for her problems.

Some manipulators start by asking you for very small favors. Called the foot in the door technique, this is a manipulation tactic that manipulators employ to get you into their servitude. The woman who asks you for a ride to work may not mean any harm, so do the favor if you want to help. But watch her carefully. Does she start asking for more rides to more places? Does she ride with you to work every morning without ever pitching for gas or coffees? Does she suddenly ask you to babysit her kids after work and housesit all weekend? A manipulator will turn a tiny favor into a multitude of big favors. Feel free to say no at any time.

Skilled manipulators may even do things for you and make it look like they are not taking advantage of you. Back to the example of the woman who asks for a ride to work, she may pay for gas to make you believe that she really just needs help and she intends to repay the favor. But soon, you are her personal chauffeur, and your time is just as valuable as gas and wear and tear on your vehicle. As her demands increase, she continues to pay for gas, making you feel confused about whether or not you should cut off the rides. Don't let small gestures of kindness make you want to serve a person like this. You can still say no and mention that your time is just as valuable as gas money.

Manipulators may also insult you to strip away your sense of dignity and self-worth, so that you continue to tolerate their ill-treatment of you. They may use barbed compliments, like "I love your hair. It looks so much better than before!" They may also pick on your insecurities so that you believe what they say about you. They will defame you to others, giving you a bad reputation and turning everyone against you in order to punish you for not doing what they want, or to ensure you don't draw strength from friends.

Finally, avoid people who always make you feel guilty. Guilt is the number one tactic employed by manipulators. They spin complex emotional webs around people, making people feel more and more indebted to them. If someone tries to make you feel guilty, remember all of the things you have done for them. Or realize that something you did to them really wasn't so bad and you deserve to be forgiven. Forgive yourself and then you won't feel the need to make someone forgive you.

For example, I had a co-worker who did me a huge solid one time. I was late on a deadline, so he stayed late after the workday had ended to help me out. Later on, he asked me to do the same for him and I happily obliged, since I felt I owed him one. However, the next time he asked for me to stay late to help him, I told him, "Sorry, I have to get home to my family for dinner."

He shrugged and said, "That's OK. I mean, I missed dinner with my family to help you out a few weeks ago, but I can't expect the same kindness from you." Guilt began to overtake me, and then I realized what he was doing. I became angry and told him to let it go, since I had already repaid his favor. I didn't let him get to me with guilt and he hated that. He refuses to talk to me to this day. But I am glad that I confronted him because I put an end to his manipulation and didn't let him take advantage of my desire to repay his kindness.

Chapter 6: Empaths, Parenting, And Raising Sensitive Children

Whether you are an empath or not, your children may be gifted. Raising them requires some care and delicacy to teach them how to use their gifts constructively and avoid the harmful side effects that can make empathy a curse.

Patience And Understanding

Encouraging an empathic child to develop his gift and acknowledging his special powers are essential parts of parenting empaths. Many people will dismiss your child's gifts throughout his life. You don't want to be one of them. If you provide your child with gentle, patient support, he will grow up stronger and happier.

Empathic children are not always easy. They may be emotional and temperamental. They may go through mood swings, as they absorb the energy of those around them. They may even act out in frustration because they don't know how to handle the influx of energetic information they receive all day long. Often, empathic children are shy and even emotionally distant. Unexplained tantrums and mood swings, particularly in public places, are hallmarks of empathic children.

When your empathic child goes through any of these trying phases, simply tell him that you love him and you are there for him. Encourage him to talk to you about what he is feeling so that you can show him how to cope with his emotions. Finally, always listen and accept what he tells you, because that way you teach him to love and accept himself.

Don't Punish Your Child For Moodiness

When your empathic child acts out, you may believe he is being defiant or behaving badly. While it is acceptable to teach him better ways to behave, you should not punish his emotional outbursts or mood swings. You should instead soothe him and ask him to communicate what is wrong.

Empathic children don't understand their gifts or where their feelings come from. They are often confused and terrified by the things they experience. Punishment only makes this worse. Being a source of stable support for your child will be more helpful.

When your child acts out, look around and see where he may be drawing his feelings from. For instance, if he is suddenly irrationally angry and yelling, ask him why he is mad. If he says he doesn't know, notice if anyone around you is angry. Then tell him, "I think you're picking up that person's energy. You're not actually angry." This helps him learn to separate his emotions from the emotional energy of others.

Teach Coping Skills

Learning coping skills from a young age can help empathic children have easier adulthoods. Always use your child's problems with empathy as a chance to teach him new coping skills.

When he gets upset, teach him to relax through breathing. A friend of mine taught her empathic daughter to wrap a blanket tightly her hands so that she felt safe. Find something that soothes your child and teach him to reach for that thing or engage in that activity when he begins to well up with feelings.

Also, keep your child active. An active empathic child is less likely to dwell on his emotions. Involve him in sports or swimming or martial arts. Physical activity will teach him how to work with a team, ground himself, distract himself, and soothe himself with healthy activity.

Stimulate your child mentally. Use educational

movies, books, and toys to keep his mind busy. Work with him on his homework. Sign him up for extracurriculars. Consider putting your child in a gifted and talented program if he qualifies, so that his mind is kept busy and challenged.

You can also sing him a song or repeat mantras when he's upset. Tell him to sing this song or recite the mantras to himself whenever he gets overwhelmed and stressed when you're not around.

You can also teach him the other tools in this book. As he gets older, you can introduce more complex tools, such as grounding or shielding or emotional freeing.

Don't Over Medicate

Many empathic children are misdiagnosed as having ADD, ADHD, depression, bipolar, or anxiety. Their gifts are treated like illnesses. The medications pediatric psychiatrists prescribe are seldom helpful. They simply numb your child and prevent him from learning to cope without medication. They may also prepare him for a life of addiction.

While this book is not encouraging you to ignore a doctor's advice, be cautious and seek a second opinion before agreeing to give your child medication. Try coping skills like breathing and play therapy with a child counselor before you resort to medication.

Being An Empathic Parent

Whether or not your child is empathic, you may face some special challenges as an empath parent. You can be more attuned to your child, but you can also worry more and take things too personally. You may place too much emphasis on your child's emotions.

It is imperative to always listen to your gut as an

empathic parent. You have better intuition than most people and you can use this to protect your child. Your child may not understand why you tell him to avoid that person or why you won't let him go to a party because you have a bad feeling. Just be patient and explain that you are an empath.

Avoid taking things your child says too personally. Especially if your child is not an empath, he or she may not place such a high emphasis on emotion. Often, his or her bad mood is not your fault. Set boundaries and try not to cater to his or her moods, or you could spoil your child.

Discipline and structure are important in raising a child. But so is doing what you think is right. Just listen to your heart and follow your gut in parenting. You can be a better parent than anyone else because of your intuition and sensitivity.

Chapter 7: Empaths And Work

Being an empath in the modern workplace can feel impossible for some people. But it is possible if you take some additional steps to help yourself. Like with everything, you must take good care of yourself and emphasize alone time to relax and detox.

Enjoy Your Work

Empaths don't do well at jobs where they don't feel that they are using their gifts or making a positive difference in the world [14]. Meaningless jobs, or jobs working for immoral people or companies, can rapidly deplete and hurt an empath. Toxic work environments with no room for growth and no recognition can hurt an empath's delicate emotional framework [14]. Finally, highly competitive jobs where people are not very nice can be difficult for empaths [14].

To succeed at work, you should seek a career you

love. If you already love your job, then you should not switch careers. But if you are unhappy, your productivity will suffer and your overall quality of life will decline.

Most empaths thrive in jobs where they can help others. They can succeed as counselors, social workers, teachers, doctors, nurses, caregivers, psychiatrists, or other helping roles. The problem is that they can take on the energy of their clients and become very depressed and burned out.

They also do well in jobs working with animals, plants, or the outdoors, since these things ground them.

A lot of empaths are creative, so they can do well in the arts.

Empaths do best when they are alone, so they can be

particularly successful in lone wolf careers, such as freelancing. Empaths can thrive in legal or accounting careers if they are able to work by themselves. They can excel in jobs involving computers, as long as they can work alone or from home. They are also excellent small business owners.

Empaths can do well in careers that use their hands, such as construction, provided that they have a positive, supportive team with caring leadership and plenty of incentives.

Empaths should probably avoid corporate jobs that don't encourage creativity and emotional support [14]. They should avoid jobs with no helping or emotional components, such as being a cashier in a major retailer or a waiter at a busy chain restaurant [14]. They probably won't enjoy or succeed at customer service or sales, particularly competitive sales roles, either [14]. Call center jobs can expose empaths to a barrage of angry customers, which can physically and emotionally wound empaths.

This does not mean that you can't do well in these roles, but you must be sure to have a hobby to clear your energy and help you make a difference outside of work so that you feel your life is still meaningful. Be sure to volunteer somewhere and do yoga before or after work to help counteract the stress of these careers.

Avoiding Burnout In Helping Professions

Empaths in helping professions can be stellar, but they can also get burned out. You must learn to clear the energy you take on from other people that you assist in your job. In fact, this burnout is known as compassion fatigue, where you suffer because of the compassion you feel and the emotions you take on from your clients [15]. Especially if you work with people or animals who have been through trauma, you can take on this trauma as your own, known as "secondary traumatization" [15].

The symptoms of compassion fatigue include but are not limited to:

- Exhaustion, both physical and mental
- Problems with relationships and intimacy
- Hypersensitivity to emotional content in the news or TV shows
- Obsession with the pain and suffering of others
- A feeling of numbness when you would normally feel compassion
- Isolation; never wanting to go out and do things with friends
- A lack of interest in your former pastimes and hobbies
- Impatience and irritation
- Drinking or other bad habits to self-medicate
- Nightmares and constant intrusive thoughts about the trauma of others
- Dread of work

When you begin to experience these things, you absolutely need to clear yourself. Self-care here is essential. Take some time off of work if you can and heal with yoga, meditation, energy healing, or even a spa day.

Be sure to keep a self-care regimen when you return to work. Continue to work out or do yoga and meditate each day. Take care of your body and eat well. Drink chamomile tea to help you sleep.

It is OK to seek therapy to work through the trauma you have picked up from other people. This trauma is like your own, so you need someone to teach you how to process it properly in your mind.

When you lend an ear or open your heart to a client, realize that you can't give him or her permanent space in your mind. After the client has gone, visualize yourself evicting the client from your mind and physically pulling his or her energy from your body. A shower or just washing your hands can help make this visualization more real to you, as it symbolizes letting go and washing yourself clean of a trauma.

Focus on joyful things when trauma intrudes in your mind. For instance, if you are reliving the horrible rape story your client just told you, turn your mind to something more wonderful, such as watching a video of puppies playing. Distract yourself from negativity with positivity.

Rely on your partner as a source of comfort and joy. Let him or her hold you and tell him or her about your day. Don't reject intimacy, even if you want to, because it is an important part of healing yourself from secondary trauma.

Treat your alone time as sacred. The few minutes between clients when you do paperwork, the commute to and from work, and some alone time at your home are all times when you can enjoy your own thoughts. Dedicate yourself to these thoughts and don't let other people, or thoughts of other people, steal this time away from you. Let people you live with know that you need some time to yourself. Fill that time with things you enjoy, such as bubble baths or good music.

Finally, avoid violent or negative movies and TV shows. Watch comedies that make you laugh. Read books that have light content. This helps you distance yourself from the pain of your job and filter out the pain of the world. It is best for empaths to avoid watching the news, as this usually only hurts them.

Dealing With Co-Workers' And Clients' Energy

Since you absorb the energy of those around you, you can become "cluttered" by the feelings of your co-workers and clients at work. The most helpful thing to do when your clients and/or co-workers get to you is to find some time alone, even in the bathroom, and practice breathing to calm yourself and let go of emotions that are not your own.

After work, don't just go home and crash in front of the TV. Take some time to unwind. Practice yoga and meditation to free yourself from the stress of the day. Whatever you do, don't continue to think about work. Chase those thoughts away by focusing on other things that are not work-related.

Be sure to have a life away from work. You want to be able to enjoy your time off without being around your co-workers even more. You can meet your co-workers for drinks, for example, but don't make a habit of it. It is OK to not want to socialize with the people you have to work with. Protecting your emotional health is more important than fitting in and pleasing others.

In highly stressful situations, practice blocking to keep others' stress at bay. Breathe throughout the situation. Excuse yourself if you must to regain your bearings.

Don't be a people pleaser. Empaths tend to spread themselves too thin, trying to make everyone happy. Think of your own happiness before you agree to take on someone's workload for the weekend or cover someone's shift. You can say no. Setting boundaries is very helpful here.

Finally, decide to have a sense of humor about work. When an angry client hurts you, decide to make a joke about it to yourself or to an understanding co-worker to make the negative energy more positive. Or find a distraction in a positive thought or funny joke after you are finished dealing with the client. Inspirational quotes and motivational mantras are great ways to make your mood more positive throughout the day.

Chapter 8: Empaths And Society

In modern society, being an extrovert with low sensitivity and high competitiveness is valued. Few people bother to understand or care for empaths. As an empath, you may feel lost, broken, and undervalued. You may feel that you don't fit in and you are condemned to a life of loneliness.

Fortunately, society is beginning to recognize empaths and say, "These people need care too!" The wealth of online resources for empaths shows that valuing and honoring empaths is a growing trend. That should lend you hope.

Nevertheless, thriving in this society can be tough. It is imperative that you take some steps to protect yourself and nurture yourself in a society that does not do it for you. You are responsible for your own happiness, so you must create it.

I often let society tell me that I was crazy. I was extremely unhappy and negative as a result. Because society didn't value me, I didn't value myself. In time, I learned to validate myself throughout the day, because I had worth and value, no matter what anyone said. I also learned to stop believing that I was crazy, regardless of how little society recognized my gifts, and seek pleasure in the fact that some people do understand how special empaths are. This helped me feel more at peace and I eventually found my wife and a core group of friends who didn't belittle me.

Set Distance From Other People

Society is full of non-empathic people. These people may intentionally or unintentionally violate your boundaries because of your natural affinity for pleasing others. Since you hate disappointing people, you strive to please them, and you don't put up a fight. Thus, people find it easy to take advantage of you, not understanding or caring how much harm they are causing.

It is easy to let other people bleed into you. As you try to help others, you take on their emotional turmoil and give parts of yourself away. You do incredible harm to yourself as a result. Soon, you can't help people anymore because you have nothing left to give. You feel exhausted, bitter, and unhappy. Now no one wants to be around you.

Putting distance between yourself and others can help you prevent this energetic taxation. Treat yourself as a separate entity from others to prevent energetic transfer. Feel someone out before listening to him or spending time around him, so that you can avoid those who bring you down or cloud your energy with negativity.

Physical distance is helpful, but so is emotional distance. Here is an example. Someone is telling you about how his dog died, and as an empath, you can feel his pain. Sitting farther away from him can help ease the transfer of sadness, but you will still feel some of it because of the emotional transference that goes along with conversation. You can put emotional distance by choosing to offer your condolences and then no longer engaging in the conversation; after all, you don't owe this person help. Or you can decide that while you are going to help this person, you refuse to feel his sadness as your own because it is not your emotion. You choose to feel happy instead by reflecting on something great that happened to you earlier in the day.

Always Put Yourself First

This society values people who adamantly and assertively ask for what they want and put themselves first. If you don't do this, then no one can be expected to simply know what you need and give it to you. You are responsible for standing up to yourself and putting yourself first, because no one will do it for you.

Consider putting yourself first as an essential act of self-care, just as critical as brushing your teeth or washing your hands after using the bathroom. Without question, think of your needs and how to get them. When you feel that your needs are being violated or neglected, ask someone to please change their behavior.

If you can do something for yourself, then do it. It is up to you to take care of yourself and your body at the end of the day. A yoga routine, a pleasurable hike, a few minutes of alone time – these are all ways you can care for yourself. Don't let other people make you give up these acts of self-care. These acts are sacred. If you want to help someone, agree to do it outside of your sacred alone time. Turn your phone off so no one can bother you. Tell your family to wait until you are finished and ask friends to make plans with you at different times.

Focus On The Spiritual

Modern society is known to be quite cold and anti-spiritual. You will get weird looks when you say that you are a spiritual person. People often value their phones more than their spirits now.

You don't have to be this way. It is OK to dedicate yourself to spiritual pursuits and growth. Whether you are religious or simply an avid meditator, you should focus on activities that connect you with yourself, Nature, and spirituality. Find a religion or spiritual pursuit that you care about and shamelessly dedicate yourself to it.

Empaths are highly spiritual people. Therefore, you need to emphasize that in your life.

Unplug From The Electronic Universe

The electronic universe of social media and online comments can be just as emotionally scarring to empaths as being around people in real life. Social media exposes you to the emotions and energies of others, as well as their hateful comments and angry political opinions. You also see lots of bad news and negativity on social media that can drain your energy and make you more negative as a whole.

It is better to unplug yourself from the electronic world. Don't spend too much time on social media. Don't allow yourself to get sucked into pointless political arguments and don't engage with ugly comments. There is far more to life than battling some stranger on the Internet, and you must preserve your precious energy for these important things.

Engage In Regular Energy Cleansing

Since society can be quite negative, you will find that you are often plagued with toxic residual energy. Just a trip to Walmart or another busy store can expose you to dark energy that hurts your emotional health.

Regular energetic cleansing is essential. You may use crystals and baths in freshwater to restore your energy balance and filter out negative energy. Or you may turn to reiki, Tai Chi, yoga, acupuncture, light healing, and other such things. Meditation and physical activity are two simple cleansing activities you can perform yourself for free.

Value Quality More Than Quantity

Lots of friends who don't care about you is significantly worse than having one friend who really cares. Quality of relationships is always more important than quantity. You want to value people who actually support you and care about you, instead of worrying about how unpopular you are and giving your time to people who squander it.

Since you have a natural tendency to attract energy vampires, you must be careful about the people you let into your life. Always get to know someone well before you invite him or her into your life and share your personal details with him or her. Don't give too much time to people whom you don't know, and don't spend too much time around them either.

It is OK to spend lots of time alone and do solitary activities. Don't feel guilty for not going out and attending every vogue party.

Maintain Your Privacy

To protect yourself from the negative aspects of society, you must value and maintain your privacy. This allows you to create a safe space where you can get away from it all. Letting people into your life invades your privacy, so you should avoid it unless you know that you can trust someone to respect your safe space.

Don't give out too much information about yourself

to people you don't know well. You don't know how they will use it. Energy vampires will use your personal details against you to hurt you, and since you are more sensitive than most people, these wounds can be difficult to heal.

Have A Healing Home Space

Your home is a safe space where you can get away from the negative energy and toxic emotional noise of society. Having a safe space to get away is essential for your success in life as an empath.

If you live with other people, you must have your own room or at least a small space that you can call your own. You must make this space ideal for healing. You might add crystals, inspirational pictures, or art that uplifts you. You might keep pets that make you feel better. You might even use soft upholstery that feels good and comfortable furniture. Do whatever you need to do to make your home space an enjoyable, private, and quiet place that makes you feel positive.

Keep your space quiet. Ask that people don't come in when you are spending time rejuvenating after a long day. Don't let people invade your space unless you invite them. You can play uplifting music that you enjoy or engage in relaxing rituals here without being interrupted.

Leave out things like TVs and phones and computers or turn them off when you are engaging in relaxation. You don't need electronic or external distractions obliterating your peace.

Chapter 9: Empath Friendships And Relationships

This is a good chapter to show someone you know who is trying to have a healthy relationship with you. This chapter is for other non-empathic people, as it deals with the nuances of maintaining a friendship or other type of relationship with an empath. From now on, "you" will refer to the person trying to build a relationship with an empath.

Empaths require a little bit of delicacy in relationships. They can love unconditionally and wholeheartedly, but they can also be hurt more easily and they can act out toward their loved ones when they are overwhelmed. They tend to take things too personally, as well. With a little finesse, you can eradicate the bad and nurture the good that comes of loving an empath.

How To Maintain A Healthy Relationship With An Empath

Empaths tend to become their partners, which can lead to an emotionally complex and even co-dependent situation. You can avoid this by lovingly setting boundaries and maintaining clear communication [15].

When you come home from a long day in a bad mood, your empathic partner will be able to tell. You can cause him or her a lot of distress by saying, "I don't want to talk about it." Be prepared to use your partner's abilities for comfort and listening by telling him or her why your day was bad. Communicating emotionally helps your empathic partner feel at ease [15].

Never expect your partner to change. Empathic abilities are wired into your partner's brain [15]. If you can't handle loving an empath, then you shouldn't be with one.

Also, don't attempt to control an empath or try to "make" him or her ignore emotions [15]. Don't dismiss an empath's emotions, either [15]. All of these behaviors deny an empath's natural personality and make him or her intensely unhappy.

Take what an empath says seriously [15]. Empaths may seem impulsive or even fanciful. They may seem like they're being dramatic or hysterical. They can't help it. When they say something, they mean it. When they have an intuition about someone or something, they are right.

Give an empath his or her alone time [15]. Don't take it personally. Empaths require alone time to recharge after being depleted all day by other people. You must also treat the empath's relationship with his or her pets as something sacred, so you should never dismiss or mistreat his or her animals, and you should never ask him or her to get rid of a pet.

Last but not least, emphasize love. You must be loving and supportive because your empathic partner needs to be lifted up. After giving himself or herself all day long, your partner is probably drained and exhausted. He or she needs to be built up and uplifted. Make him or her laugh, show him or her physical affection, and make an effort to make him or her smile with sweet gestures. Empaths love romance and being wooed because usually they are the ones doing the wooing.

Setting Healthy Boundaries

Empaths hate setting boundaries and disappointing the people they love [15]. They also shy away from conflict and the emotional maelstrom it causes them [15]. Thus, it is your job to gently but firmly set boundaries.

Once you tell an empath your boundaries, he or she

will want to respect them to make you happy. An empath's number one goal is your happiness, so don't take that lightly. You don't need to yell or nag at an empath to get him or her to respect you. Just tell them what you need, and they will deliver.

Encourage the empath to tell you his or her boundaries. Sit down and ask, "Let's have a discussion about boundaries. What do you want? What do you need to feel happy?" This way, the empath feels comfortable setting boundaries, without fearing your reaction.

Encourage peaceful conflict that drives results and solutions, instead of fighting with the empath. Empaths hate fighting. You can keep your voice calm and avoid pointing fingers as you work together toward solutions to issues in your relationship.

When you are feeling bad, avoid taking it out on the empath by yelling or throwing a fit. Instead, calmly tell the empath how you feel. The empath will gladly listen and try to help you feel better. The same goes for insecurities [15]. Don't cast your insecurities onto an empath and fight about them; simply tell the empath what you are insecure about.

Achieving Balance

Most empaths have no idea how to achieve balance within themselves. Hence, their relationships can be unhealthy and imbalanced. Furthermore, most empaths have been used and broken before, and they have deep trust issues that can make their relationships more tumultuous or hot and cold.

Being a rock for your empathic lover is a good way to counteract and balance his or her frenetic emotional energy. As empaths are highly emotional, they often take solace in partners who are more emotionally stable and probably non-empathic. While this can create problems in that the two partners don't always see eye to eye, it keeps the relationship balanced.

If you are a stable person, then be sure to be so for your empath. Anchor him or her by listening and providing logical rationalizations when he or she gets emotional. Offer support, instead of dismissing his or her feelings. Never ignore his or her intuition, as it is most likely spot-on.

However, if you are also empathic, there are a few additional things you can do to strike balance.

HSPs With Non-HSPs

An HSP is a highly sensitive person, and empaths are HSPs. Non-HSPs can balance and ground empaths, but they can also be a bit obtuse regarding how empaths feel [16].

I know this firsthand, since my wife is a non-HSP and I am an HSP. We make it work by letting our differences balance us. The only way a relationship can work between an HSP and a non-HSP is if both are accepting of each other.

HSPs often don't speak up. It is crucial for the non-HSP in the relationship to take notice of that [16]. Instead of just putting on your music first thing in the morning, ask your HSP partner if he or she wants to listen to music. Instead of talking because your HSP partner is not saying anything, ask if he or she wants quiet time or a conversation. Let your HSP partner speak by asking him or her questions.

HSPs always fear that they are burdens [16]. Hence, you must make it clear that you love your partner. Provide plenty of reassurance, even if your partner doesn't ask for it. When your partner appears sad, insecure, or moody, just offer a loving hug or hold your partner's hand. These little gestures can mean a lot.

You may not understand why your partner hates going into the grocery store or flips out when a sad commercial plays. You don't see the logic or need for such emotion. But your partner can't help it. You have to be willing to accept his or her sometimes odd, inexplicable behavior without saying, "Don't be like that" or "You're being ridiculous." He or she is going through things you can't understand, so don't assume you are right in dismissing his or her experiences.

Understand that your partner is probably introverted and can't handle tons of social gatherings [16]. You may want to go out every other night, but your partner can only handle it once a week. Your partner feels like a burden and does what you want, which taxes him or her. You should have a social life apart from your partner and make it clear that you don't mind if your partner comes along or stays at home.

During a conflict, let your partner have a time-out to collect his or her thoughts and feelings [16]. This is not stonewalling. Your partner is simply overwhelmed and hates conflict. You can bring the issue up again at a later time in a calm, non-threatening tone.

When Both Of You Are HSPs

It may seem that two HSPs are the ideal match. While they certainly can be, both of you must take care to keep balance and set boundaries in the relationship. Otherwise, you will both be lost.

The two of you can create something amazing because of your shared ability for empathy. Enjoy that and let it be the strength of your relationship. But remember, relationships require give and take. As you both try to give all you can, one of you has to be willing to take. Creating balance is essential so that you both receive gratification from giving and support from taking.

The sex, conversations, and sharing can be stunning. You can both love the same things and appreciate your need to be alone at times. You can also both understand each other, almost as if you are one being, not two separate beings. Communication will flow easily.

But bad moods can be contagious and you can create a very negative environment [17]. When one or both of you are upset or picking up on bad vibes, take some distance from each other. Try to regain positivity with happy thoughts, meditation, or an enjoyable activity before you spend time around your partner again.

Physical pain can also be shared. If you are suffering, encourage your partner to clear before and after spending time with you. Use your partner as a source of healing and strength. Do the same when your partner is in pain.

There is no ability to hide things in this relationship [17]. Your partner can read things you are not ready to share, and vice versa. If you need your privacy, acknowledge that your partner has read you and say that you just aren't ready to talk about it. If you read something in your partner, don't bring it up. Let your partner tell you in his or her own time.

Chapter 10: Challenges For Empaths

Beyond the challenges covered in this book, here are some common challenges that empaths encounter and how to fix them.

Odd Sleep Patterns And Insomnia

Empaths tend to have trouble sleeping because of emotional stress [18]. They also struggle with insomnia, particularly when something bad happens or they are suffering from depression [18].

The key here is to have a relaxing and cleansing bedtime ritual to prepare your mind for sleep. Do things that relax you, instead of taking in more energy. Be alone and meditate. Do some yoga. Drink some chamomile tea. Soak in a luxurious bubble bath.

If you still can't sleep, try taking melatonin, a nonhabit-forming chemical that your brain produces to bring on natural sleep. Stay up reading a good book or doing crafts until the melatonin kicks in.

Adrenal Fatigue

Adrenal fatigue occurs when high levels of emotional or physical stress tax the adrenal glands over the kidneys [18]. The glands become unable to stop producing cortisol, the stress hormone, in natural ways. Thus, your sleep is disturbed, you gain stubborn weight despite no changes in diet or exercise, and you feel tired all of the time except late at night [18]. You may also have skin issues and hair loss and you may feel depressed or low-spirited [18]. In extreme cases, adrenal fatigue can lead to other health problems, including kidney failure, and severe unexplained weight loss [18].

It is best to reduce stress to avoid or heal adrenal fatigue. Supplements like vitamins, magnesium, and cortisol blockers can help reduce symptoms. Don't engage in rigorous exercise, which increases cortisol and adrenaline, and instead focus on light enjoyable exercise, such as dancing, swimming, walking, biking, gentle hiking, or yoga. Definitely avoid toxic house products, BPAs in plastic, and processed food. Avoid the keto diet, as it has been shown to increase stress [19]. Also, avoid alcohol, marijuana, and caffeine, as all three spike cortisol during or after consumption [19].

Overall, the only ways to really cure adrenal fatigue include getting enough sleep, eating whole foods, and cutting out stress by taking some time to yourself each day and cutting out electronics and negative people [19]. If you keep feeling stressed, you will perpetuate the cycle.

Maintaining A Healthy Diet

Empaths don't always eat well. They get overwhelmed and don't feel like cooking. However, they can absorb the suffering of the animals they eat and they can respond worse to chemicals in processed foods than other people. They tend to get sicker from eating bad diets.

It is imperative to eat well. A vegetarian or vegan diet may be helpful for your sensitivity to the suffering of animals. If you do eat meat, seek free-range poultry, grass-fed beef, and wild-caught fish. Replace processed food with easy to prepare whole foods, like whole grain bread and raw cheese. Limit eating out and frozen foods in favor of whole foods. Eat lots of vegetables, even consuming baby carrots for snacks. Non-GMO veggies are ideal.

Physical Health

Empaths must take extra care of their physical health. Because of the emotional-physical connection, your emotional sensitivity can wreak havoc on your body [6]. This does not mean that you have to be sick. You can enjoy great health and longevity, as long as you make yourself a priority, work to reduce stress, and avoid negative people or situations.

Addictive Behaviors

Treating and avoiding addictions is crucial for any empath. Empaths tend to engage in addictive behaviors, which only worsens their mental and physical health. Seek immediate treatment for addictions and find healthier alternatives to destructive pleasure-seeking or self-medicating behaviors.

Mental Health

Empaths are at an increased risk for depression, anxiety, and other mental disorders. This is explained by the high number of emotions they absorb throughout the day, as well as social rejection and alienation.

To stave off mental illness, be sure to do things that

relax you and make you happy. Counseling can be helpful. Avoid medication unless you feel as if you have no choice for relief. Medication can dull or numb your natural gifts.

Discernment

For highly intuitive and sensitive people, empaths tend to have very poor discernment skills. The short explanation for this is that they ignore their gut feelings and obvious red flags because they believe everyone deserves a chance. As they work hard to accept and understand everyone, they let some people in who don't want to be helped. They also tend to forgive things that should not be forgiven, simply because their capacity for empathy is too strong.

It is best to be hard-hearted, so to speak, when it comes to new people. Ensure someone really wants and needs help. Also, determine if a person actually deserves your help, or if he or she has a long history of screwing people over. Protecting yourself is important because you can't help everyone and squandering your gift on people who don't deserve it leaves nothing left for people who really do deserve to benefit from what you can offer.

Chapter 11: Empaths And Communication

Empaths can be excellent communicators because they are so empathetic. They can read body language like FBI interrogators and sense what the other person is *not* saying. They are also helpful and compassionate, and they love to listen.

The only barriers empaths have to good communication include shutting out brain chatter or "noise," overcoming shyness, and avoiding rambling. If you can overcome the barriers you have in communication, you are free to become the best communicator on Earth.

Shy Vs. Silent

Some empaths are shy, it's true. But most are simply silent because they are too busy listening. Both characteristics can make other people overlook you or even ignore you. Your self-esteem and ability to make new friends can suffer as a result.

Therefore, it is best to practice injecting yourself into conversations. If you speak up, others will listen. Follow the flow of the conversation and volunteer relevant ideas, stories, or jokes. Think of something interesting to say to someone. All of these things can get you out of your shell so you are less shy or silent.

Rapid Speech And The Solution

When you feel inundated by emotion and hence nervous, your speech tends to be rapid. Other people may have difficulty following you. Slowing down is imperative for smooth communication.

The best way is to offer pauses now and then. As you feel yourself running out of breath, or as people stare at you with their eyes wide, pause. Apologize for getting excited.

Also, pause between phrases or between topics. This is logical and helps others follow.

By articulating each syllable of a word, you naturally slow yourself down. But it can be hard to do this when you are nervous. Take a deep breath and focus on the words you are saying. Possibly visualize them written on paper in your mind as you read them aloud.

Look people in the eye as you talk. You can clearly see their reactions to your words. This gives you a chance to see when you are losing your audience, so you can reign it in.

Rambling And The Solution

Your mind is abundant with ideas. Therefore, you tend to ramble as you attempt to verbalize all of your intense emotions and thoughts. Other people may get bored and lose focus as you talk. This can be frustrating.

To avoid rambling, first be mindful of how much time you are taking up in a meeting or conversation. If you have been going on for several minutes, consider taking a pause. Let other people share ideas. Then, you are able to find new things to talk about that appeal to the whole group.

Also, lower your voice when you make a certain point. This is a trick that I learned from school. Instead of raising your voice or using more words, deliver your message in a low, slow voice. This can give your speech more deliberation and power, as you are able to pick out the right words.

Finally, plan your words before you speak. Have a plan for what you say. For instance, think of an opener, how to make your point in a few words, and finally how to summarize it. Think of important words; more unusual words will stick out in your memory. That way, you don't have to fumble for the right words and ramble on.

Here is a good framework: point (your main point), reason (why the point is valid or helpful), example (illustrated how your point works in other situations), and summary (wrap it up neatly in a few words).

Direct Conversation

Empaths can struggle with being direct because they fear hurting someone. However, direct conversation is crucial when you are keeping up healthy relationships.

One way to do this is to practice when the stakes are low. For instance, if someone left his laundry on the floor, you can politely ask him to pick it up. The stakes are low because this issue is not terribly personal. As you have more conversations like this, you will find it gets easier.

Practice talking only about facts. Most people respond better to facts than to emotion. Back to the laundry example, don't talk about how the laundry upsets you because you require neatness to feel organized, as the other person is not likely to care about that. Instead, mention how laundry all over the floor can pose a tripping hazard, how spiders can hide in the clothes, and how it is harder to do laundry when it is everywhere instead of in a basket.

Ask direct questions. "Why do you do that?" is vague and will likely elicit an "I don't know" response. Instead, ask, "How do you think this helps?" By asking someone questions, you make them reconsider their actions and arrive at solutions on their own.

Use lots of "I" messages. "I feel that this is not ideal." Then back your "I" message up with a clear explanation as to why you don't agree with something. Propose a new solution and say, "We can work on this." By saying "We" you invite collaboration, which most people respond to well.

One-Sided Conversation

You listen so much that you find yourself in one-sided conversations often. The other person speaks for hours, never asking you questions or inviting you to speak. When this happens, you must practice being direct and inserting your own words into the conversation. You have to force your way into one-sided conversations.

Find a relevant reply and state it, talking over the person if necessary. If a person continues to ignore you, you may consider leaving the conversation.

Brain Chatter And The Solution

The brain chatter, or "noise," that you take from others' emotional energy can be distracting in conversations. This is where mindfulness comes in handy [20]. By practicing mindfulness in conversation, you focus totally on the conversation and block out the unhelpful chatter cluttering your brain.

Mindfulness is so powerful that you can use it to overcome the pain of cancer and other chronic diseases [20]. Hence, it follows that it can help you tune out brain chatter. The key is to focus on the conversation, paying attention to the sights, sounds, and other sensations. When brain chatter intrudes, acknowledge it but then turn your attention back to the sensory details of the conversation at hand. You effectively teach your mind to pay attention to conversations without entertaining brain chatter and other distractions.

Power In Speech

Empaths often don't have much luck asserting power in conversations. They often feel guilty about asserting themselves and prefer to give power to others. But especially in work situations, no one takes you seriously unless you use power in speech.

The first key to taking power involves speaking in a loud, firm voice [21]. Only then do people look up. You should also speak first and refuse to stop talking when someone else does. Make your point efficiently but don't stop until you are finished making it.

Complaining And The Solution

When your world is filled with negativity, you tend to complain. This can make you seem like an overly negative person, which can repel other people. It can also darken your mood and create a habit that you perpetuate every time you speak.

Lighten things up. When you feel like complaining, decide to seek out the silver lining or one positive aspect of something too. For instance, if you are complaining about the rain, remember how it is keeping the temperatures cool or watering the flowers you enjoy in the park.

Diminished Communication And The Solution

Most relationships fall apart due to diminished communication. Over time, you both get so distracted and wrapped up in your own issues that you fail to communicate anymore. You may see more fighting or long, awkward lapses in conversation as a direct result of this.

When this happens, you can use your empathic gifts to spark communication again. Pay attention to your partner and glean clues about what he or she is feeling. Then bring it up. "I notice you seem tense. What is wrong? I want to help."

You can also remember things your conversational partner loves talking about. Bring them up. Ask him about an event that recently happened or mention current affairs. Find a topic that you know interests him and gauge his response. If he doesn't seem interested, find a new topic until you land on the one.

I Have Something Important To Say

When you have something important to say, don't feel afraid to say it. You may hang back, fearing that someone won't care or won't want to hear what you have to say. But what you have to say matters too.

Start by taking a deep breath to relax. This moment may not be as stressful or worrisome as you think it is. Clear your mind and speak aloud, "I have something important to say."

Then, begin speaking without waiting for permission. Say what you have to say in a short but efficient way. Focus on the facts. Use an emotional appeal if you think the other person will listen.

Chapter 12: Empaths And Boundaries

What Are Boundaries

Boundaries are simply your personal rules. They can range from "I don't have sex on the first date" to "You can't talk to me like that."

Empaths are easily impressionable. Thus, they tend to take on the values and boundaries of the person they are spending time around. This erodes their own. They are willing to bend or ignore their own boundaries just to please someone else. This is why psychopaths and narcissists and borderlines tend to take advantage of empaths.

Having a core list of values is crucial to keeping your own identity and setting boundaries. By having these values set in stone, you can tell people to respect them. As you do this in relationships, you avoid getting hurt. But you also make your partners and friends happier because they have clear guidance on how to act around you. Normal people don't react poorly to boundaries; they actually appreciate them, so don't worry about hurting peoples' feelings.

Empaths And Boundaries

Setting boundaries is so important to conserving your energy and protecting yourself from energy vampires and regular non-empathic people. With boundaries, you can recharge. Boundaries are ultimately an act of self-care.

No one will know what your boundaries are unless you tell them. Give people a chance to make your relationship stronger by setting boundaries. In the early years of my marriage, I didn't set boundaries and thus my wife would get upset because she couldn't figure out how to treat me. When I learned that it was OK to set boundaries, our relationship fell in line and became more supportive.

People who refuse to respect your boundaries are dangerous people, and probably energy vampires. It is an important clue when someone refuses to respect your boundaries or argues with you over a boundary. Avoid this person and don't give them too much more of your time.

Allowing Boundaries

Allowing boundaries is imperative to any relationship. You must respect when someone tells you that he or she is uncomfortable with something. Similarly, you must do the same.

Analyze how you feel. Also, analyze the past and things that upset you before. These things give you important clues about where you stand and what you value. Then, you can tell a person when you first meet, or you can tell someone when he or she comes close to violating a boundary.

Most people have a few shared boundaries. They don't like being stolen from, called names, or physically abused or hurt. But that is pretty basic. There is way more that you probably don't like. For instance, do you like that creepy dude coming onto you, or that woman talking to you 24/7 so that you can't get work done? These are some examples of where you should allow yourself to set up boundaries to stay comfortable and preserve your energy.

Remember, give yourself permission to set boundaries. No one will do it for you. And you have the right to be reasonably happy in life. Don't let people violate your boundaries left and right.

Boundaries Vs. Stress

Not having boundaries can increase your stress, which you already struggle with. You get stressed as people inundate you with their energy and fail to respect your energy or time. You get stressed as you try to figure out if you are overreacting or not. And you get stressed as you try to think of how to stand up for yourself.

Furthermore, you may bottle up your emotions. As someone keeps hurting you, you eventually have enough and snap. This can create a lot of stress and a rift in the relationship with the person you exploded on. Handling the matter more calmly early on is essential to avoid this.

Take some time to de-stress. Breathe, meditate, do some yoga, go to your happy place. Then, reflect on the event. If it still bothers you, then it's important. From your place of peace, think about what you can say that won't create a fight. Plan a tactful and calm way to set the boundary without yelling or swapping nasty names.

Steps Before Creating Boundaries

Before creating a boundary, you must get comfortable

with giving yourself permission to set boundaries. You must cement the idea in your mind that you deserve to be comfortable and reasonably happy. You must remind yourself that you are responsible for your own happiness, since few people are as intuitive as you are.

Go through this mental process whenever you find your boundaries violated or hurt. Give yourself the permission and encouragement required to do something about the situation at hand.

Action Steps To Boundaries

The first step to setting boundaries is recognized that you feel somehow violated, bothered, or hurt. Don't just dismiss this emotion. You have a right to feel that way. If it hurts you, then it's a big deal.

The second step is determining to do something about it. You can't keep letting someone make you feel this way. You have the right to stand up for yourself.

The third step is practicing what you are going to say. You don't want to say anything hurtful or accusatory. You don't want to erupt in anger or raise your voice. Practice being firm but unwavering. State your needs clearly, how you feel when someone violates your boundaries, and what you want in the future.

Role-Playing

To practice assertiveness, you can practice with yourself in the mirror. Practice how to speak up for yourself.

If you have a friend or therapist, you can practice setting boundaries in a role-play scenario. Role-playing is so helpful because it demonstrates how a real-life scenario will play out. This teaches your brain to approach reality in the same manner.

Stand Up And Say It

Role-playing and practicing in a mirror helps...but it does not actually set boundaries for you. It is time to stand up and say what you need. Practice with role-playing and then confront someone.

I had to do this with a friend. While he is a great friend, he felt free to help himself to my drinks and food without asking whenever he came over. If I ordered something at a restaurant, he would just reach over and seize food off my plate. Not only was this really rude, but I didn't appreciate him mooching off of me. But I was scared to upset him.

So, I practiced what I would say with my wife one day before I knew I was having dinner with him. Then I stood up and said it. When I saw his hand inching onto my plate, I said, "I don't appreciate it when you always steal my food."

He looked hurt. But he quickly accepted it and apologized. He added that my food just looked better than his dish. I then offered a solution: I would split my meal with him as long as he gave me half of his. The compromise worked out great and he respects my boundaries now.

Standing up to him scared me. But in the end, it went better than I expected. That gave me more confidence to confront other people about bigger issues, such as my mother about her overbearing treatment of my wife. As a result, people began to respect my boundaries. Most of them never even knew that they were bothering me.

Is Yes To Someone Else, A No To You?

Some people have very different boundaries from you. This hardly means that you should question your comfort levels and boundaries. It is OK to be different.

Maybe my friend doesn't mind when someone helps himself to his food. But I mind. I can't let this make me feel that my boundary is not important. Other people are different from you and probably don't allow things you do, so find your boundaries and stick by them, without letting others guilt or manipulate you by pointing out how someone else is fine with something you are not fine with.

Chapter 13: Empath Toolbox For Navigating Energy

Being an empath can be hard. That's why there are various tools you can use to make life easier.

Grounding Exercise

This simple grounding exercise can help you gain control when you are suffering from cluttered emotions or indiscernible distress.

Start by planting your feet firmly on the ground, preferably bare earth [22]. Now imagine roots emerging from the soles of your feet, anchoring you to the ground.

Now, lay on your back. Breathe in and imagine the air filling your lungs as light. Breathe out the negativity within you. Imagine yourself melting into the floor [22]. Become one with the earth and hold the position for a while.

Empath Gifts

Love yourself by remembering all of the wonderful gifts you have:

- Intuition
- Sensitivity
- Ability to read people like books
- Ability to distinguish lies from truth
- Ability to tell how things will turn out
- Ability to feel things no one else can
- A propensity for healing
- Creativity
- Unique perspective
- Willingness to go against the trends
- Ability to handle being alone
- Love for animals and Nature

Empath As Rescuer

You are a rescuer by nature. Others can exploit this and you can give too much of yourself, however. Always consider how important it is to take care of yourself, or else you won't be a good rescuer.

Before rescuing someone, consider if it is really your job. Can you expend the energy now? Is this person asking for help, or do you just want to help? Is this person known for using and abusing others or taking advantage? Does this person often ask for help, only to resort to the same old habits?

Only rescue people that really want to be helped and want to get better. Always be discerning. Furthermore, remember that each person is responsible for his or her own life, so you cannot fix everything for them. You can lend a helping hand, but don't try to heal them entirely. That is beyond your power.

Energetic Exchange

The energetic exchange between you and other people is powerful, allowing you to give yourself and take on parts of another person. While this can be beautiful, it can also be very harmful as you bleed into another person or let a person steal your identity away.

To prevent this energetic exchange, consider blocking negative energy. Take some time to yourself away from people to cleanse yourself.

Envision your chakras. Your heart chakra is particularly vulnerable in empaths. Imagine filling your heart area with love and light. Then imagine shutting a door on it. This prevents you from engaging in harmful energetic exchange.

You can also perform cord-cutting. This is covered later.

Energy Drain From You And Others

Throughout the day, you will feel drained because other people are able to take your energy and fill you with their own exhausting negativity.

To conserve your energy, you absolutely must take some time to yourself away from others [18]. Do something you love. Care for your body.

You should also take some time to restore your energy. You can do this by filling your home with crystals, or by bathing in fresh running water. You can also do it by practicing yoga and imagining yourself breathing in positive energy, while expelling negative.

Always have pets and plants in your house. They can revitalize your energy, too.

Numbing Out And Dealing With Distractions

One common problem is becoming overwhelmed. You become numb as you grow used to the inundation of emotional energy from others. You also let yourself get lost in distractions in order to block out the pain of your daily energetic troubles.

Take some time to meditate and get in touch with your real feelings. You must acknowledge the things you are blocking out. Mindfulness is useful to clear out distractions, so that you can feel your true heart's contents [20].

Tools

Raising Frequency

Each person vibrates at a particular frequency of energy. Higher frequencies tend to repeal lower, more negative frequencies. Raise your frequency can help you stay positive and stave off negative people or situations.

Start by avoiding negative situations and people, as they lower your frequency. Try to replace anger, hatred, and other negative emotions with more loving, positive ones.

You can raise your frequency by eating raw, whole foods and organic food. Drink herbal tea and take herbal supplements that were lovingly prepared. Gardening can also help you do this. Taking a walk-through Nature, standing in the rain, and taking care of house plants can do this, as well.

Keep crystals in your home. Crystals are high energy and raise your vibration. Magnets and magnetic jewelry can do this, too.

High Energetic Resonance

The energetic vibrations of the world can be quite damaging and taxing to empaths. Hence, you must find sources of high energy to resonate with. Otherwise, the world itself will drain you.

Keep your vibrations high. Surround yourself with positivity and lovely things. Inspire your happiness. This will help block out the overall negativity of the world.

Love Resonance

Just as negative emotions resonate within you, so do positive ones. It just depends on which you choose to focus on. Resonating with love can magnify its wonderful effects for you.

Be sure to surround yourself with love. A simple red painting of a heart can be sufficient. Watching romances and reading them can help, too. As long as you keep your mind on love, you can resonate with it.

Plus, as you love yourself, you continue to increase the resonance of love in your spirit. Take care of yourself and list good things about yourself. Remember at least three things that you are grateful for each day. All of this will resonate love within you.

Meditation

Meditation is always critical, especially for empaths [22]. It allows you to clear your mind and heart of distractions and other people's energy. Find a meditation app on your phone or look up guided meditations. Attend a local meditation group. Engage in meditation at least once a day.

Also, practice mindfulness throughout the day. When you are doing the dishes, for instance, focus only on that task. This teaches you mental mastery and control [20].

Stones

Stones have high vibrational energy locked inside of them. Hence, having them in your home can provide a useful source of energetic boosting and cleansing.

Here are some great crystals for your home:

- Black tourmaline
- Tourmaline
- Amethyst
- Black kyanite
- Hematite
- Rose quartz

When using crystals, you can hold them and imagine them absorbing the negative energy from within you. Keep them near you as you meditate or ring them around you to assist with your meditation.

You can also find crystals that match the colors of

your chakras and line them up down your body, with white such as quartz for your head, amethyst for your third eye, blue sapphire or some other blue for your throat, green such as malachite for your heart, yellow or gold like citrite for your solar plexus, and red such as red jasper for your sacral. This will naturally balance and cleanse your chakras.

Spiritual

Unlike most people, you have a high spiritual calling. You will function better and feel happier if you focus on this. Let yourself find your spiritual calling. Add spirituality for your life in any way that you can. Prioritize it over the physical and material parts of life.

Blocking Negative Energy

To truly protect yourself, you can block out negative energy. Whenever you go out, imagine yourself surrounded by a shield or armor that deflects negativity. Pray to your deity of preference to please slay all negativity and protect you.

When you encounter a negative person, reaffirm this. Imagine sending their energy back to them tenfold in the form of love and light. Refuse to accept dark energy.

Don't listen to complainers or entertain manipulators. Decide that you are too good for that negativity and move on. Clear yourself after the exposure.

Also, clear yourself often if you work in health care or some other helping profession. You absorb negativity from your clients and must release it to be healthy. Keep crystals in your office, drink herbal tea, and quickly cleanse after each client and then engage in a longer cleanse after the workday.

Shielding

Always shield yourself from others. The best way to do this is to envision yourself covered in a great shield, or a pyramid of light.

You can also use physical distance to create a shield. Separate yourself from a harmful or toxic person by stepping farther away to lessen the energetic effect. Go to another room to separate yourself with a wall if you can.

Cord-Cutting

A cord-cutting ceremony is a great way to cut the energetic ties you share with other people, particularly harmful or draining people [22].

Visualize the energetic cord that connects you two. It may be thick and colorful, or white, or black. Whatever it looks like to you is a representation of how the cord works.

Now imagine that you are snipping the cord with big scissors or a knife. As you snip it, all of the energy and feelings you have for the person pour out of you and along with the cord that you are returning to them. It is all gone. You no longer have their energy within you.

Clear your body and your environment. Refuse any more contact with the person to keep another cord from forming.

Clearing-Releasing

Throughout the day, you must clear and release energy from your body to feel well. Otherwise, you take on everyone's energy and feel terrible. You begin to lose yourself.

Start by taking a bath. As the water falls from your body, envision it taking negative energy with it. Now, close your eyes and ask that all negativity leave when you exhale. Hold your breath, letting the energy collect, and then release it. When you breathe in, picture light filling your body. Feel it tingling and filling you with joy as it spreads from your scalp to your fingertips.

Clearing Your Environment

To clear your environment, you can use smudging [22]. Burn a bundle of white sage and walk around the perimeter of your house with the windows and doors open. Let the smoke drive out negative energy. Visualize the smoke collecting bad energy and driving it out.

You can say a mantra like, "I ask all negative things to leave my space." Drive this mantra with meaning. This only works if you mean it! Claim this space as your own and banish anything that doesn't belong.

You should smudge and clear your space at least once a week as an empath. Some empaths do it every day. I find it helpful to do it when I clean.

Living near water or having a source of running water in your house, such as a fountain or clean fish tank, can help circulate energy, as well.

Chapter 14: Forgiveness

Since empaths are highly sensitive people, they tend to suffer from more hurt and emotional devastation than others. They often unwittingly place themselves in victim situations, as they attempt to heal harmful people and lose their identities and boundaries in relationships. The result is that you might have extra emotional baggage as an empath, and you must learn how to forgive those who have hurt you.

Just as you feel things more richly than most people, you can experience pain and suffering at the hands of others in a more piercing manner. This can make forgiveness particularly challenging. However, forgiveness is necessary for your emotional well-being and your growth as a person. Do it as an act of self-care.

What Can You Gain By Forgiving?

You can gain immense physical and mental benefit

from forgiveness [23]. Forgiveness releases emotional stress that you hold in your body, effectively lowering blood pressure, improving your immunity and healing responses, and decreasing anxiety and depression [23]. It works beautifully to make you feel better.

You can gain health by forgiving, but you can also regain your identity. Instead of dwelling on the past and what someone has done to you, you reclaim your present and your happiness. You stop dedicating time to someone who doesn't deserve it and then you have more time and emotional energy to care about things you love.

What Does Unforgiveness Cost You?

Unforgiveness can cost you the ability to heal. As you hold onto the negative emotions brought on by someone, you continue to feel them and suffer their consequences. You can become consumed with anger, hatred, and other emotions that give rise to depression. You can lose sleep.

Lastly, life just isn't pleasant if you are always stuck in the past. You fail to move on and embrace the present. You may turn down great people because you hold onto trust issues; you may fail to be happy because you are too busy thinking of how much you hate your past.

Forgiveness Vs. Unforgiveness

Forgiveness is a release of emotions that you continue to process after a hurtful event has happened. Unforgiveness is where you hold onto the emotions for a long period of time, not healing and reliving the pain over and over. It is obvious which one is better.

Forgiveness can be hard. You may not feel that someone deserves to be forgiven. But this is an act of self-care for yourself, not for someone else. The person who hurt you doesn't even have to know that you have forgiven him or her and moved on. Only you need to know.

Forgiveness does not mean that you start talking to someone again or let someone back into your life. It means that you stop thinking about the person or event that hurt you and embrace a more positive present and future. You begin to live your life as you should, instead of living locked in the past.

Furthermore, forgiveness does not equal forgetting. When you go through a painful experience, you learn something. Always hold onto that lesson and strive to prevent the same from happening again. But you don't need to dwell on the lesson and its painful implications over and over. That is not helpful at all.

Forgiveness Saved My Life

I had trouble forgiving my family for the emotionally harmful environment they raised me in. I spent every day thinking about how my family had hurt me, reliving the experience over and over and never healing. I would often lose sleep because of the memories that played over and over in my head.

When I was diagnosed with high blood pressure, I was devastated. I was only thirty-five, dealing with a lifelong health problem! But when I learned about the connection between forgiveness and blood pressure, I decided to go through the forgiveness process. At my last doctor's appointment, my blood pressure was in a safe range. I don't even have to take drugs to keep it down now.

I'm also happier. And I feel less stressed. I get better sleep and no longer battle depression. I believe that without forgiveness, I would still be miserable and on the road to a heart attack. Forgiving my family let me move on and get healthy. It saved my life.

How To Know If You Need To Forgive

You can tell forgiveness is in order when you experience the following issues:

- You think about a bad event more than once a week.
- You lose sleep over it.
- When you see someone's picture or hear his or her name, you feel a flood of negative emotions.
- You question your value and have poor self-esteem.
- You make decisions based on what someone said to you or did to you a long time ago.
- You feel afraid to move on in life.
- You have nightmares or intrusive thoughts about something that hurt you.
- You obsess over something that happened in the past, feeling the emotions over and over.

Forgiveness And Equilibrium

Forgiveness is key to establishing your equilibrium,

or balance. You cannot feel balanced when you are constantly reliving pain from a past event. You also can't feel true happiness and live your best life if you are trapped in the past.

Forgiveness And Relationships

Picture this scenario: your spouse cheats on you. You decide to stay with him or her. But the pain of the cheating constantly afflicts you, leading to constant fights. You don't trust your partner and constantly watch him or her. He or she resents the watching and fighting and begins to rebel by drifting further and further away from you or even cheating again.

Now, when someone hurts you, it is never your fault. But it is your fault if you choose to keep a relationship with the person and continue to dwell on the past. Neither of you will be happy or able to move on and make actual progress.

Forgiveness is imperative to any relationship. It doesn't make much sense to dwell on the past if you want to stay with someone. You have to let it go to embrace a better present.

How To Forgive

Forgiveness starts with the decision that you have had enough of a painful memory or grudge. Once you have made that decision, you have already begun the process.

When you reflect on the event that hurt you, don't focus on blaming the other person. Instead, understand that you feel hurt or angry or whatever you feel. Let yourself feel this. Then tell yourself, "I am responsible for this emotion."

When you go to sleep, refuse to fill that time with dwelling on your hurt. Remind yourself to think of positive things that relax you. As your thoughts drift to your hurt, breathe out and acknowledge how the thought makes you feel. Then envision releasing it into the air with your exhalation. Now, find a more positive thought unrelated to the memory.

Decide to flow like water. You can't change the past. So, you must flow into the future, making life work regardless of what has happened to you. Visualize yourself letting go and flowing forward.

If you played some role in a negative experience with a person, take responsibility for it. Don't blame yourself or feel stupid. Just think that the other person is not as much as at fault as you have previously thought. This can help you let go.

Finally, list five positive qualities about the person you can't forgive. This helps you overcome solely negative feelings toward him or her. It is helpful to realize that no one is black or white, meaning that no one is all bad or all good.

Write him or her a letter, describing how you feel, how you decided to forgive, and how you see value in the person still. You may not give this letter to the person, but you will find that writing your feelings down is cathartic. You can burn the letter, save it for when you need reinforcement for forgiveness, or send it to the person who hurt you. Do whatever makes you feel better.

To truly make letting go real to your mind, you can write down the memory or the person's name. Then burn it. Visualize your feelings dissolving with the flames and blowing away with the smoke and ash.

Forgiveness Affirmation

An affirmation can help you forgive, too. Tell yourself repeatedly, "I forgive [insert name]." Do this whenever unforgiveness begins to fill your mind and heart. It teaches your brain to think of forgiveness instead of reflecting on the emotions that you hold onto.

How To Tell When You've Completed Forgiving

You know that you have completed the act of forgiveness when you no longer dwell on the memory day in and day out.

You can also tell when you start to fall asleep, without thinking of the memory.

You know you have forgiven when you stop engaging in revenge fantasies. The thought of destroying someone's car is no longer a source of satisfaction to you.

You will start to move forward in life. You will have more time and energy for yourself and the things you want to do. You may even start dating after a bad break-up or make a new friend.

A final sign is when you see someone's name or picture. You will no longer feel hatred or anger seize your heart. Instead, you will feel calm acceptance.

Conclusion

Being an empath is a gift. You have the ability to heal people because you understand what is wrong. You are able to become an extremely healthy, intuitive romantic partner because you are sharply attuned to your partner's feelings and needs. You can also be a thoughtful and considerate friend. You are sensitive, so you can care for yourself better than other people can. You may even have psychic gifts that help you protect yourself and protect others.

However, being an empath does come with a special set of challenges. Mitigating these challenges help you unlock your gift with a minimum of suffering. Don't view being an empath as a curse. It is simply a part of your identity and a gift that you can use to better yourself and better the world.

Society undervalues empathy. This is a sign we are actually more powerful than we're taught to believe. We have stunning capabilities that we fail to recognize because we are told we are just too sensitive and we need to toughen up.

With the techniques in this book, you can utilize a robust toolkit to lessen the bad side effects of being an empath. You can enjoy a life of joy, even when you absorb negativity from the world around you. Getting rid of or ignoring your gift is not helpful; it is part of your brain structure and who you are. Instead, you can learn how to live with your gift and make it less negatively impactful.

From learning to shield energy to setting boundaries, you can restructure your interactions with the world to take care of yourself. Remember, you are not good for anyone if you are taxed and stressed by the energy of other people. Putting yourself first and taking care of yourself is a priority that will ultimately help everyone around you, too.

A life of joy, optimism, and peace is possible for

empaths. Now that you have read this book, you are prepared to enjoy the rest of your days more completely. I know this is possible, as I have accomplished it myself.

Resources

[1] Marsh, Abigail. The Fear Factor. 2017. Basic Books. ISBN-13: 978-1541697195.

[2] Reiss, Helen. The Science of Empathy. Journal of Patient Experience. 2017, Vol 4, Issue 2, pp. 74–77. doi: 10.1177/2374373517699267.

[3] Cornell Education. Modeling Six Universal Emotions. https://people.ece.cornell.edu/land/OldStudentProjects/cs490-95to96/HJKIM/emotions.html.

[4] Yan, Weng-Jin, Wu, Qi, & Chen, Yu-Hsin. How Fast are Leaked Facial Expressions: The Duration of Micro-Expressions. 2013. Journal of Nonverbal Behavior. Vol 37, No 4. DOI: 10.1007/s10919-013-0159-8

[5] Jung, Carl. Archetypes and The Collective

Unconscious. 1981. Princeton University Press. ISBN-13: 978-0691018331.

[6] McCraty, Rollin..Impact of a Workplace Stress Reduction Program onBlood Pressure and Emotional Health in Hypertensive Employees. Journal of Alternative and Complimentary Medicine. 2003. Vol 9, No 3, pp. 355-369.

[7] Depression: recognizing the Physical Symptoms. WebMD.
https://www.webmd.com/depression/physical-symptoms

[8] Orloff, Judith, MD. Emotional Freedom. 2010. Harmony. ISBN-13: 978-0307338198.

[9] Nummenmaa, Lauri, et al. Bodily Maps of Emotions. Proceedings of the National Academy of Sciences. 2013. DOI:

https://doi.org/10.1073/pnas.1321664111.

[10] Wilson, Sylia, et al. Interpersonal Dysfunction in Personality Disorders: A Meta-Analytic Review. 2018. Psychology Bulletin. Vol 143, Issue 7, pp. 677-734. doi: 10.1037/bul0000101.

[11] Kiehl, Kent & Hoffman, Morris. The Criminal Psychopath: History, Neuroscience, Treatment, and Economics. Jurimetrics. 2011. Vol 51, pp. 355-397. DOI: https://www.ncbi.nlm.nih.gov/pmc/articles/PMC4059069/.

[12] Ruocco, Anthony, et al. Subjective Cognitive Complaints and Functional Disability in Patients With Borderline Personality Disorder and Their Nonaffected First-Degree Relatives. 2014. Canadian Journal of Psychology. Vol 59, No 6, pp. 335-344. DOI: 10.1177/070674371405900607.

[13] Ni, Preston. 14 Signs of Psychological and Emotional Manipulation. 2015. Psychology Today. https://www.psychologytoday.com/us/blog/communication-success/201510/14-signs-psychological-and-emotional-manipulation.

[14] Orloff, Judith, MD. The Best and Worst Jobs for an Empath. https://drjudithorloff.com/the-best-worst-jobs-for-an-empath/.

[15] Gulla, Ashley. 15 Things to Remember if You Love an Empath. LifeHack. https://www.lifehack.org/articles/communication/15-tips-help-you-love-empath.html.

[16] Mosciki, Meredith. The Challenges of Being an HSP in a Relationship with a Non-HSP. Highly Sensitive Refuge. https://highlysensitiverefuge.com/hsp-and-non-hsp-

relationship/.

[17] Winter, Catherine. When Two Empaths Fall in Love. A Conscious Rethink. https://www.aconsciousrethink.com/7781/when-two-empaths-fall-in-love/.

[18] Orloff, Judith. The Empath's Survival Guide. 2017. Sounds True. ISBN-13: 978-1622036578.

[19] Mayo Clinic. Adrenal Fatigue: What Causes It? https://www.mayoclinic.org/diseases-conditions/addisons-disease/expert-answers/adrenal-fatigue/faq-20057906.

[20] Shapiro, Shauna & Bootzin, Richard. The Efficacy of Mindfulness-Based Stress Reduction on Sleep Disturbance in Women with Breast Cancer: An Exploratory Study. 2003. Journal of Psychosomatic Research. DOI:10.1016/S0022-3999(02)00546-9.

[21] Williams, M. The Speech Act Method. University of Sheffield. https://www.sheffield.ac.uk/polopoly_fs/1.71421!/file/mike2.pdf.

[22] 10 Spiritual Clearing Techniques for Empaths and Sensitive People. Restore Emotional Balance. https://www.restoreemotionalbalance.com/energy-clearing-techniques.html.

[23] Tutu, Desmond, Dalai Lama, & Abrams, Douglas. The Book of Joy: Lasting Happiness in a Changing World. 2016. Avery. ISBN-13: 978-0399185045.

Evolving Empath

How To Move Past Your Limitations And Live A Fulfilling Life

By

Joseph Salinas

Introduction

The word Empath is being used more and more often today in memes and articles about emotions and relationships and popular psychology.

Do you know what an Empath is? Do you suspect you may be an Empath but are not sure? Are you an Empath whom struggle with handling so much emotion and energy? Are there tried and tested solutions out there that can help the empath not only cope, but evolve and thrive?

In this guide, we unfold all the secrets to the world of the Empath and answers all your questions and more.

Written by an empath and highly experienced personal effectiveness coach, specializing in the psychology behind emotions and decisions, and how to live life to the fullest.

Explore the science behind it all, learn about the pros and cons of being an empath, the different types and how to handle all that input.

Learn how to use psychological models and tricks to ground yourself, and how to grow and evolve as an empath.

Learn how to step outside your comfort zone to live your best life

This guide will change your perspective forever. It will make you more self-aware, keep you grounded and knowledgeable in the ways of the empath. It will assist you in clearing out the emotional garbage and negative emotions surrounding you, save you from toxic personalities, emotional vampires and dark triad personalities. It will help you chart a path for yourself to evolve

Thousands of readers have been able to change the course of their lives by implementing these strategies, and so can you!

Start reclaiming your life and passions today - don't let another person tell you that you are 'too sensitive' or should 'develop a thicker skin'. Be done with chronic emotional exhaustion and toxic relationships for good!

Read it now to give you the emotional freedom you crave!

The Scientific Understanding Of Being An Empath

What Is Empathy?

According to the Dali Lama, "Empathy is the most precious human quality". Generally defined as the 'ability to understand and share another person's emotional state, it is a multidimensional construct, consisting of cognitive and emotional components' (1), as well as behavioral aspects.

Trying to understand another's perspective, and how their experiences, biases, personalities, priorities, and concerns have shaped their perspective, is the process of empathetic listening. It is more than just sympathy, which is the ability to support others with compassion.

Whilst the 'capacity to feel and share the emotions of others (2)' is the most frequently used definition of empathy in social-cognitive neurosciences, which basically means it is seen as an affective state, with emotional reactions, caused by emotional sharing, it is not strictly emotional.

A broader definition states that empathy is a feeling that "enables to access the embodied mind of others 'in their bodily and behavioral expressions', irrespective of the content (emotions, sensations, actions, etc.) of the others; lived experience (2)". Thus, recognizing:

- Higher-order cognitive functions that underpin self-other distinction
- Conflates sympathy and empathy, which
- Share basic processes, such as autonomic processes and feelings
- Share outcomes such as pro-social behavior and moral development

Differences Between Empathy And Sympathy

Empathy consists of 'feeling into', and sympathy 'feeling with' someone else. (3)

The feeling describes one's mental awareness of the physiological and bodily states and changes (4) triggered by the perception of others'

- motor,
- somatosensory,
- emotional,
- affective or
- intentional lived experience.

The difference between empathy and sympathy relies upon three key components of bodily self-consciousness:

- self-identification (the experience of owning a body),
- self-location (the experience of where I am in space) and
- first-person (ego-centered) perspective (the experience from where I perceive the world) (5).

These distinctions are important to understand how important the awareness of being outside the other person and having to reach him is as a prerequisite for empathy.

Empathy thus has three core components:

- disembodied self-location (enabling to mentally put oneself into the other's body)
- hetero-centered visuo-spatial perspective-taking (coding for the others' visuo-spatial perspective) and
- parallel coding of one's body position in space (ego-centered).

This enables *feeling, thinking and understanding* what the other (as other—not me) is feeling and thinking from his/her own viewpoint and lived experience.

Thus, 'feeling into someone else' requires a clear understanding and awareness of one's ipseity (self/individualism) so that the other appears in his/her alterity (6) (otherness).

Thirioux defined empathy then as:

"Empathy is the capacity to feel and understand the emotional, affective but also motor, somatosensory, or intentional experience of others and their associated mental state, while adopting the others' visuo-spatial perspective and psychological viewpoint and consciously maintaining self-other distinction." (7)

Why Is Empathy Important?

Empathy facilitates pro-social behavior, enables parental care and attachment, and plays a mitigating role in the inhibition of aggression.

Researchers such as Daniel Goleman (8) and others

have shown that emotional intelligence and empathetic ability (a key part of EQ) is far more important than intellectual ability in long term success.

A study by the Center for Creative Leadership on Empathy in the Workplace concluded that:

- Empathy is positively related to job performance.
- Empathy is more important to job performance in some cultures than others (9), placing an even greater value on empathy as a leadership skill.

With fifty percent of managers seen as poor performers, according to a Gentry poll, the development of appropriate leadership skills such as empathy is crucial.

In some professions, such as the caring professions (medical and nursing personnel), where connection and compassion are crucial to the well-being of patients, empathy is taught as a subject (10), and studies have shown that interventions can be successful in raising levels of empathy. (10) Dr. Helen Riess from Harvard Medical School states: "Empathy is undergoing a new evolution. In a global and interconnected culture, we can no longer afford to identify only with people who seem to be a part of our "tribe." As {we have} learned, our capacity for empathy is not just an innate trait—it is also a skill that we can learn and expand."

Therapeutic empathy is regarded as an essential component of communication in health care training and is now taught in many countries including the US, UK, and South Africa. (12)

A crucial aspect of therapeutic empathy is to hold on to self:

Empathy is openness to oneself (why do I feel odd about the way he is looking at me?) as well as openness to the other (why is he doing that?).

It is a form of knowledge but also a skill that can be practiced and mastered. It consists of observation, listening, introspection, and deliberation. This is repeated in cycles as required to come to a conclusion.

This cognitive process acknowledges competing interests in a *respectful nonjudgmental way*. 'Its manifestation is that of the provider being fully present but *without the emotional complications of concern or pity*." (13)

This implies showing high levels of cognitive empathy, as well as emotional empathy and empathic concern without resorting to absorbing their pain and emotions. Thus, empathy allows emotions to be managed in a socially positive way.

By this definition, it should protect health professionals against burnout, yet we have more than half of those surveyed reporting signs and symptoms of burnout, and it may be because they have not learnt how to manage empathic feelings.

Empathy levels differ between cultures – there is the old Native American proverb 'never judge a man until you have walked in his moccasins'. The higher the value placed on individualism in a society, the lower the general abilities to display empathy (14).

It is about more than just understanding the viewpoint of someone other than you, it is about the ability to communicate more effectively: understanding their models of the world, what matters to them, what words to use or avoid. (8)

Three Types Of Empathy

Daniel Goleman describes the 'empathy triad' as

three forms of attention in his book on attention (10):

Cognitive Empathy

A natural curiosity about another person's reality

- Ability to see the world through other's eyes
- Pick up cultural norms quickly
- 'Theory of Mind' or 'Mentalizing' are often used synonymously.
- People with strong cognitive empathy may engage in:
- Tactical/strategic empathy - the deliberate use of perspective taking to achieve certain ends (11)
- Fantasy – tendency to identify strongly with fictional characters
- Perspective-taking – spontaneously adopt other's psychological perspectives (11)

Emotional Empathy

- Feel what the other person does

- Instantaneous body-to-body connection
- Tuning into their feelings
- Pick up facial, verbal and non-verbal signs
- Depends on tuning into our own body's emotional signals, which mirror the other person's feelings
- Chemistry, sense of rapport, referred to as the 'we circuitry' or being in the 'bubble of we' by Daniel Siegal, UCLA psychiatrist.
- Watching others receive painful shocks showed clear activation in the same areas of the brain during brain scans, indicating a simulation of the other's experience.

Empathetic Caring

- Expressing caring about another person
- Possible to have both cognitive and emotional empathy but not express empathetic caring.
- Heart-to-heart connection
- Partakes of the brain's circuitry for parental love.

Somatic empathy refers to the physical reaction you feel when you empathize, probably due to the mirror neuron response in the somatic nervous system.

What Is An Empath?

Whilst there is a lot of controversy relating to the actual definition of an empath, a simple contemporary definition is that of being *hyper-empathetic*. There is no definitive research explaining why some people feel more strongly than others, however, there are several theories posited and empathy itself is the subject of many research endeavors in psychology, neurosciences, and philosophy.

Highly Sensitive individuals sometimes have a special ability to sense what people around them are thinking and feeling. Survivors of early childhood abuse or later traumas often develop hypervigilance, which is a state of 'always being ready for fight or flight' responses, but it does lead to being hyper-aware of the thoughts and feelings of those around you.

Psychologists often refer to someone that experiences a great deal of empathy as an empath, and in some spiritual circles, it has a deeper connotation of someone with psychic abilities in sensing the emotions of others. Some refer to sharing energy or absorbing energy on behalf of others.

If you viewed empathy as a spectrum, as it is not only one construct, but multiple levels, empaths would be on the higher end of the spectrum. They show enormous compassion for others, but easily get drained emotionally from just simply feeling too much.

Is It Genetics?

Understanding the science behind empathy, it is clear

genetics play some role in empathy and hyper-empathy or being an empath.

Specific genetic studies have pointed to the arousal of the amygdala when shown arousing images (13) in individuals with specific gene variants. Other variants pointed to the ability to read emotion, sensitivity to negative emotional information (13), level of social skills and self-esteem.

Many experiments have shown that empathy to some extent can be taught, and an understanding of epigenetics will clarify the changes environment and other influences can have on a person's genetic make-up.

Many believe that developmental and environmental influences play a major role in the development of empathy in children, such as relationships, parenting style, parent empathy, prior social experiences and how we learn to deal with aggression.

There is no definitive research that conclusively points to why some people are empaths and others not, but there are some studies that have pointed in specific directions, such as mirroring, dopamine sensitivity, personality type, and others.

'Could a greater miracle take place than for us to look through each other's eyes for an instant?'

Henry David Thoreau

Why Do Empaths Feel Things More Strongly Than Others?

Some Reasons For Empaths Feeling So Deeply

Emotional Contagion

Considered to be the initial proof that empaths do exist, emotional contagion is described as the phenomenon that individuals often feel and express the emotions of their companions (11). The Mexican Wave is a good example, or one baby triggering an avalanche of crying babies in a nursery. Empaths pick up extreme emotions very quickly, which will overwhelm the empath eventually, thus necessitating setting tight boundaries.

Increased Dopamine Sensitivity

Dopamine is a neurotransmitter associated with the pleasure response and sensitivity levels have a genetic link (12). Many empaths are also introverts and they have shown higher sensitivity to dopamine than extroverts, so will need less dopamine to feel happy.

Mimetic Desires And Mirror Neurons

Mirror neurons are brain cells involved in compassion (13) and allow us to mirror another's feelings, as described by Girard (14). It appears that the empath's mirror neurons are hyperactive.

Electromagnetic Fields

Judith Orloff, controversial researcher and author (15), states that the HeartMath Institute found electromagnetic fields generated by the heart and brain transmit people's thoughts and emotions, and claims that empaths have stronger responses to these, as well as those of the earth and sun.

Mirror-Touch Synesthesia

This relates to the amazing ability to pair two senses in the brain, for example hearing music when you look at a specific colour or to ascribe a taste to words.

It also explains the ability to feel another's pain or emotions (16).

Sensory And Affective Links

Some studies show modulation between the affective links between an empath and their subject, in as far as the brain structures activated by pain is concerned. Higher affective links with high state empathy scores resulted in increased pain perception (17).

Fear Factor

Abigail Marsh (18) recruited anonymous kidney donors (what she calls the care-based ultimate altruist) to test how they respond to other's emotions and found heightened amygdalae activity in their brains when shown fearful facial expressions (19). It can be argued that care-based altruists are highly empathetic, and she showed higher levels of humility in this group, however, her research was limited to the altruism factor.

Sensory Processing Disorder

Empaths often describe their experiences as very similar to having SPD, which is an interesting paradox, in that many people on the ASD spectrum (Autism) experiences Sensory Processing Disorder, yet they are supposedly low on the empathy scale (20). Studies have shown the type of stimuli to affect the secondary somatosensory cortex (SII) in that facial expressions of pain had higher reactions in neurotypicals, but no difference was shown with images of mangled limbs (21)

"It Is Both A Blessing And A Curse To Feel Everything So Very Deeply."

David Jones

Why Everyone Has Different Physical Tolerances

Different types of empaths have different ways of interacting with the world. Physical tolerance for socializing appears to be linked to different personality traits.

There are two brain regions – the medial prefrontal cortex and the temporoparietal junction – that is important for empathic processing. Increased brain activity in these two areas is associated with empathic accuracy, according to neuroimaging and behavioral research (31). They found this activity associated with two underlying facets of the personality dimensions Extraversion and Agreeableness.

The Big 5

Psychological, behavioral and neuropsychology researchers often refer to the 'Big 5', or the Five Factor Model to evaluate the core traits, or dimensions, of an individual's personality. Whilst many personality trait theories have been researched the FFM seems to produce the most consistent results across multiple cultures, and each of these domains represents a range between two extreme ends of the continuum, with most people lying somewhere in between the extremes (30). Big 5 tests are scored in percentages.

Most people display two to three or more of these traits, with one or two being more dominant.

These broad trait dimensions include:

Openness

This trait features characteristics such as imagination and insight.

- High - tend to have a broad range of interests, are more adventurous and creative. They are open to trying new things, focused on tackling new challenges, loves thinking about abstract concepts.

- Low - much more traditional, resist new ideas, struggle with abstract thinking, dislike change. They are not very imaginative and do not enjoy new things or experiences

Conscientiousness

This dimension features high levels of thoughtfulness, with good impulse control and goal-directed behaviors, individuals that are organized and mindful of details.

- High - Will spend time preparing, pay attention to details and finish important tasks right away. Enjoy having a set schedule
- Low - dislike structure and schedules, procrastinate on important tasks, not good at taking care of things and makes messes. Fail to return items where they belong, or to complete tasks they have responsibility for

Extraversion

Characterized by excitability, sociability, talkativeness, assertiveness, and high amounts of emotional expressiveness.

- High - outgoing and gain energy in social situations. Enjoy being the center of attention, like starting conversations, feel energized when around people and say things before thinking. Enjoy meeting new people, find it easy to make new friends and have a wide social circle
- Low – introverted, more reserved and expend energy in social settings. Dislike being the center of attention, prefer solitude and feel exhausted when they are required to socialise a lot. They hate small talk, find it difficult to start conversations and carefully think things through before they speak.

Agreeableness

Includes attributes such as trust, altruism, kindness, affection, and other prosocial behaviors.

- High - tend to be more cooperative. Feel empathy and concern for other people, have a great deal of interest in others, care about others and enjoy helping and contributing to the happiness of others.
- Low – tend to be more competitive and even manipulative. Take little interest in others, don't care about how other people feel and have little to no interest in other people's problems. Insult and belittle others.

Neuroticism

Neuroticism is a trait characterized by sadness, moodiness, and emotional instability.

Individuals who are high in this trait tend to those low in this trait

- High - experience dramatic mood swings, anxiety, irritability, and sadness. Worry about many different things and experience a lot of stress get upset easily.
- Low - Emotionally stable and resilient. Deal well with stress, do not worry too much and rarely feel sad or depressed.

Commonly used acronyms to remember the five traits are:

- OCEAN (openness, conscientiousness, extraversion, agreeableness, and neuroticism)
- CANOE (conscientiousness, agreeableness, neuroticism, openness, and extraversion)

Empaths typically score high on Agreeableness and lower on the Extraversion scales, however, some extraverts can be empaths too.

It is important to understand the difficulties with

physical limits when you are low on the Extraversion scale, i.e. an Introvert. Introverts have to find solitude and spend time in nature to recharge, their energies get depleted in social situations very quickly. And because they feel so deeply, and are intuitively attuned to other's feelings, they tend to take on much more emotional baggage and negative energy from others than their bodies can handle, leaving them exhausted, confused and disoriented from time to time.

We need to account for individual levels of empathy as well – it is not a single unipolar construct, but as we can see in the scales above, it is a set of constructs on a scale from high to low.

Individuals that are very high on the empathy scale, and very low on the extraversion scales, will have more severe challenges coping with the emotional, psychological and physical demands of being an empath, being available for people to spill their life stories to, being a good and caring friend, and often, in the work-place, being a caring colleague or caregiver.

'In essence, not every individual responds equally and uniformly the same to various circumstances.' (30)

We can measure levels of empathy with a variety of psychological tools developed over the years – psychological research on empathy has grown tremendously in the last few decades.

Many commonly available tools on the internet have no scientific backing to them and were designed to attract followers to blogs and social media. A crucial component of measuring empathy is to ascertain the maturity of the 'self-other' construct if it is to be useful.

These two of the better-known versions measure the

different aspects of empathy and is best applied in combination testing:

- The Empathic Concern scale - it assesses "other-oriented" feelings of sympathy and concern
- The Personal Distress scale – measures "self-oriented" feelings of personal anxiety and unease.

Combining these two scales helps to expand the narrow definition of empathy and will reveal those that may not be empathetic. (31)

Are You An Empath?

What Are The Characteristics Of An Empath?

Empaths are affected by other's energy and emotions and have an innate ability to perceive others, intuitively feeling what they feel, plan or think.

Empaths share many common traits, such as:

Highly Sensitive

Empaths are particularly highly sensitive individuals, whom can sense other's energy and emotions, without anything being communicated. This energy may be positive or negative.

Absorb Emotions

They act like human sponges that absorb other individuals' emotions, and carry their joys or sorrows with them. They feel their emotions as if it is their own. This may apply to someone close by or far away, that they have connected with.

Highly Intuitive

A very highly developed intuition is a trademark of the empath - they are highly intuitive about people's intentions and hidden agendas and will often detect a sense of unease when around someone that is masking.

They can also intuit when for instance a person is sad but presenting a gregarious and happy front in a social gathering.

At times their 'knowing' seems to be deeper than just intuition.

Greatest Friends

Empaths make excellent friends – you could not ask for anyone more loyal and caring. They will stick with you through trials and tribulations and defend your honor to the nth degree if needed.

They normally have small social groups with very special friends, but the more extravert could have larger social circles.

Great Listeners

Because they are such great listeners, empaths tend to draw people to them that needs to unburden themselves, and often end up with virtual strangers confessing their most intimate secrets to them.

Their friends value their listening skills and compassion. They excel in the healing and teaching professions.

Generous And Extremely Compassionate

Empaths are generous to a fault, with their attention,

their compassion, their big hearts and their ability to convey that they truly understand what you are saying or experiencing.

They are very warm and altruistic individuals and will endeavor to assistant anyone that requires their help, whether it is someone that is disadvantaged, in pain or ill, or being bullied or abused.

They are highly tolerant and understanding and will put up with much more unfair treatment than the average person.

It is because of this openness and willingness to serve and support that they are so easy to take advantage of.

Highly Tuned Senses

Empaths have highly tuned senses in that their five senses work overtime – they are extremely sensitive to sights, smells, light, sounds, tastes, and sensations. This serves as a gift when you are so aware of your surroundings and can appreciate them for making the world so much brighter, however, as always, too much can be debilitating.

At times this manifests as Sensory Processing Sensitivity and an overload of sensory signals may overstimulate them, create anxiety and confusion and lead the emotional exhaustion.

Others may present with Sensory Processing Disorder symptoms and become completely overwhelmed, leading to sensory meltdown.

Alone Time

Empaths, like most introverts, often need alone time, to recharge their batteries and replenish their resources. They often need to be replenished in nature and will benefit from outdoor activities, whether it be a sedate walk in the park, or a long hike, or simply putting your bare feet on the grass. Other times they will need to participate in water-related activities as they find that very soothing, such as a soak in the bath, a solitary swim or other watersports.

Avoid Big Crowds

Empaths will always avoid big crowds, all the shoving and pushing, smells and noise can become overwhelming very quickly. Even if they do engage, they will excuse themselves earlier than socially acceptable to find a quiet spot.

Easily Hurt

As empaths are most commonly introverted, but with huge hearts that give freely, it is very easy for them to have their feelings hurt – by unkind words, acts or omissions. They can be emotionally labile, for seemingly no reason, but it is because they are carrying such a heavy emotional and psychological load of other's baggage and karma.

They are not scared of intimate relationships but will approach them very differently to the average person. They can find intimate relationships intimidating and may be afraid of losing their identity.

Know If You Lie

Empaths have an uncanny ability to know if you lie to them or twist the truth to suit your agenda. They can sense dishonesty and discomfort or trying to hide something no matter how big or small the lie.

They can sense sarcasm and humor used as coping mechanisms to hide sadness or anger, they know when you are selfish, prejudiced, jealous, self-destructive, angry or trying to hide something.

Take On Other's Problems

As empaths will often take on other's problems as their own, no matter the consequences to their own priorities or health, they do from time to time become overwhelmed by negative or painful emotions such as anger or anxiety

They may at times feel like they are drowning in other's emotions and become emotionally exhausted easily.

When emotionally depleted they may suffer from physical and mental exhaustion.

Dark Triad

Empaths are often targeted by the dark triad personalities, especially narcissists. They may fall for their false-self presentation and be drawn into their web of deceit and manipulation, as their only wish is to heal the damaged soul presented to them.

Self-Care

Empaths are often extremely hard on themselves and find it difficult to set boundaries to help protect themselves from becoming depleted and stressed out.

They are typically not very good at emotional self-care and can easily become victims of emotional burnout.

Loved By All – Emotional Connections

Apart from being loved by friends for their gregarious warm natures, kids are naturally drawn to them and they typically have the ability to connect with animals at an emotional level.

Predict Events

Some empaths have the uncanny ability to predict certain events, without any prior or special knowledge about them.

In A Professional Capacity

In the workplace they (9):

- show interest in the needs, hopes, and dreams of other people
- are sensitive to signs of overwork in others
- are keen to assist those with personal problems
- convey compassion toward anyone who has suffered a personal loss.

Different Types Of Empaths

Most empaths lean more strongly towards one type however, there is often overlap and one type does not exclude the other. One can have affective and cognitive empathy and feel empathic caring, and in fact, people with all three abilities make excellent teachers, caregivers and leaders.

Physical

Physically receptive empaths will experience the physical sensations the person they are with is experiencing. If the person is ill, they will actually feel the physical pain that person is feeling.

Intuitive

Intuitive empaths can discern specific feelings and emotions surrounding a person or event very clearly, often talking about a 'sixth sense' or an intuition that something is not as stated, or that something will happen or go wrong. These intuitions can make them very anxious and stressed. They are exceptionally good at telling when people are lying or omitting details.

Emotional

Emotional empaths literally feel the emotions of the person they are connecting with, without that person saying anything at all. For example, if the person is sad, the empath will have a sense of immense sadness themselves.

If they can get the person to talk to them, the person will leave feeling much better, and the empath will be left holding all those negative and painful emotions.

The emotional empath is the most commonly found empath and is really the few types of empath rooted in science. Neuroscience recognizes cognitive and affective empathy.

Telepathic

These empaths may be able to discern the thoughts of another person, without any spoken communication between them. It is not always clear thoughts but only a sense of what is on their mind.

Mediums

Also known as spiritual empaths, they may feel a connection to other spiritual realms or the deceased, and they feel physical and emotional symptoms from this connection. Some even have a visual component.

Many believe that they can talk to ghosts, or it could be angels or archangels, or other beings that exist in the outside of this material world. They can feel their energy, sense them or even smell them.

The Native Americans refer to the Heyoka empath whom acts as a spiritual medium between physical and spiritual worlds. They often heal with humor and acts as a mirror to show others what they need to see.

Nature

Nature empaths can sense the energies of nature, in plants animals and in geomancy the earth. They can detect changes in nature and the effect it has on the world's nature. They know instinctively how to take care of nature, such as plants or animals.

All About Clairs

Claircognisance is often an extreme example of intuitive empaths and is sometimes referred to as 'psychics' in general discourse.

There has been no scientific proof of any clairvoyant abilities or traits, and many people have been conned by charlatans claiming to be clairvoyant or psychic. A cognitive empath with no emotional empathy could possibly participate in conning and deceitful behavior, an emotional empath would find that too painful to contemplate.

Exceptional observational skills (for example, such as found in the hyper vigilant) combined with extreme empathy may give the impression that a person can discern things the average person cannot. Very strong cognitive empathy will allow the person to tap into the other's personality and reasoning and understand their intent. The popular TV show The Mentalist is a great example of this ability.

How To Figure Out Which Type You Are

You may have recognized some of the traits described above in yourself. You may wonder, do I have cognitive empathy only or emotional, or am I perhaps a clair? So much of the explanations above resonate with me. How do you figure out which type you are?

There are numerous psychic empath tests available for free on the internet, the problem is to find which are actually reliable and which are just a light-hearted attempt at getting clicks and readers in this era of social media marketing.

Of course, the only reliable test of your empathy levels can be performed by a psychologist, preferably a neuropsychologist, whom will have a whole battery of tests available, but may rely on a particular sample from experience.

Becoming more self-aware is a good place to start:

- Keep a small journal on you, or use Notes on your smartphone
- Record every instance where you have strong feelings about another's energies.
- For example, you visit a friend, you feel their inner sadness, but they are chirpy and talkative.
- Make notes of your feelings, the exact circumstances of the meeting.
- Wait a few days and discuss it with your friend
- You may find they have had time to process some of that sadness and is now willing to talk about it.

- If you watch a speech or a person of interest, and you feel very strongly that the person is not saying what they really want to say, or that there is intent in their minds that is different to their words, make a note of the context, and your thoughts.
- Follow up to see if your feelings and intuition was correct.
- If you sense energies that you cannot explain and believe they are outside of this realm, make notes of what you sense, in as much detail as possible. Do some research about places where you sense this, to ascertain if there is merit to what you experienced.
- If you find that your empathetic feelings are seriously depleting your resources, or that it is threatening your health and wellbeing, make an appointment with a psychologist to get some clarity for yourself.
- Take care of yourself first and foremost.

Being An Empath

Empaths, Intuition And Extraordinary Perceptions

Dr. Judith Orloff, author of The Empath's Survival Guide, offers this short quiz (31) to evaluate whether or not you are an empath:

Ask yourself:

- Have I been labeled as "too emotional" or overly sensitive?
- If a friend is distraught, do I start feeling it too?
- Are my feelings easily hurt?
- Am I emotionally drained by crowds, require time alone to revive?
- Do my nerves get frayed by noise, smells, or excessive talk?
- Do I prefer taking my own car places so that I can leave when I please?
- Do I overeat to cope with emotional stress?
- Am I afraid of becoming engulfed by intimate relationships?

According to Dr. Orloff, "If you answer 'yes' to 1-3 of these questions, you're at least part empath. Responding 'yes' to more than three, indicates that you've found your emotional type."

This quiz is a very basic tool – if you look at the types of empaths and the exercises to determine what type of empath you may be, you will get a clearer picture.

Intuition plays a big role in the lives of empaths, and very often when that intuition is ignored or suppressed, they find themselves in difficult situations wishing they had paid heed to that nagging feeling.

Intuitive empaths often struggle with extraordinary perceptions, their spiritual connections, and what is sometimes referred to as second sight.

Whilst there is no scientific evidence of telepathy or clairvoyance, many intuitive empaths can testify to experiencing, for example, a searing pain in their chest, at the exact moment a loved one passed on in an accident on the other side of the world, when they have had no way of knowing that. Or suddenly waking up at night with a start, knowing full well that something bad happened to your child, without knowing what exactly, but then anxiously waiting for that terrible phone call.

Many of them will fight this extraordinary perception, refusing to talk about what they 'see' or experience, for fear of ridicule and being accused of 'attention-seeking' behavior.

Dr. Judith Orloff, author of several books on being an empath, and an Assistant Professor of Psychiatry, claims to have been born with 'second sight', and cutting-edge knowledge of intuition, energy, and spirituality. Her works have helped many empaths navigate their gifts in a way that promotes self-care and helped them understand why they feel so different, however, her writings on extraordinary perceptions have labeled her as very controversial and not 'scientific' in the academic community that she is supposed to be a member of.

The Gift Of Being An Empath

Being an empath is a gift. Empathy is a wonderful trait to have and will smooth personal interactions throughout your life, and tipping the higher end of the scale endows you with gifts not many people possess. They are open to physical, emotional and psychological information that is mostly inaccessible to the average person. These gifts are non-confrontational and can be used for the greater good and empaths should hone their skills in these gifts throughout life.

The gift of being an empath includes:

- They are naturally curious about everything around them, and when grounded and centered in themselves, will enjoy life to the fullest. They love to travel and meaningful experiences.
- They make the most wonderful, loyal friends, no one could ask for a greater gift than an empath friend. Their warmth and compassion touch the lives of all around them and leaves them feeling replete over the long term as their sense of purpose is fulfilled.
- They are great listeners, and will thus be privy to many great, deep and sad stories from all walks of life, giving reassurance to the storyteller that they are going to be fine no matter what happens.
- They are loved by children and animals and often form very strong emotional bonds with them, leading to a much enriched life. They love communing with nature and appreciates the gifts of life around them, every sunrise or flower or sunset, which assists with engendering mindfulness.

- They make strong leaders, great visionaries and can easily convince their followers to do the right thing, behave ethically and will often chart new courses and conquer new markets or ideas
- They have good working relationships due to their caring and compassionate natures, and their ability to understand other's points of view. This minimizes stress in the workplace.
- They adapt easily to working with or living in different cultures – Psychologists refer to a 'false consensus effect' (26) which basically means that because people are familiar with their own beliefs and opinions, they greatly overestimate the number of people that share them, which is an egocentric bias in social perception and attribution. This cognitive bias is due to the availability heuristic (what comes to mind quickly is seen as significant) and makes them blind to cultural differences, which can lead to misunderstandings, anger and negative discourse. Empaths, on the other hand, can pick up easily on cultural differences

and have an uncanny ability to understand different points of view and beliefs.
- They excel in the healing and teaching professions, as they have caring and nurturing natures
- They are very big-hearted people (but sometimes give too much), have passionate and deep relationships that are soul-satisfying and enriching
- Their highly tuned senses and intuition is great for negotiations or eliciting the truth from scared or traumatized people
- They are emotionally intelligent, a particularly valued skill in the competitive workplace today.
- They are dreamers and idealists that can see the big picture, even when paying attention to the detail of someone's story. They can be extremely creative, which lead to rich and fulfilling lives.

The Dark Side Of Being An Empath

Does empathy lead to compassion fatigue or satisfaction? It seems to be time-dependent, intense feelings have been linked to fatigue in the short term but to satisfaction in the long term (22) for most, for others, there have been correlations to burnout.

The ability to recognize another's perspective and thinking beyond yourself is a valuable attribute, however, for the empath, this may become toxic if not managed properly.

Some of the negative issues related to being an empath include:

Feeling Drained After Spending Time Around People

Empaths expend emotional energy to socialise, and especially introverted empaths will need to muster all they have to participate in social activities, make small talk and listen to people tell them far more than what is socially acceptable. They will often feel the need to leave social gatherings after a couple of hours, in order to find some solitude to unwind and recharge.

Confusing, Disorienting, Exhausting

When empaths are engaged in a lot of socialising over a period, with no break to recharge and work through the muddle of emotional and psychological baggage they have picked up along the way, it can easily leave an empath confused and disoriented. This is particularly true when the empath is not skilled in handling the incoming loads and does not have a clear sense of self-other.

They will wonder why they feel so exhausted, and sad maybe, especially if they do not intellectually believe they have something to feel sad about, not understanding that they have picked up the sadness and emotional pain from people they have been in contact with. They may wonder what is wrong with them, why they cannot shake those negative feelings when they have so much to be grateful for.

Feel Other's Physical Pain

Feeling others' physical pain can confound issues even more. Not all empaths will feel physical pain, but those who do can find it very disturbing to experience another's physical pain in their own bodies.

Hate Interpersonal Conflicts

Empaths hate interpersonal conflicts with a passion – it makes them extremely uncomfortable, to the point of experiencing anxiety and physical pain.

They will do anything to avoid interpersonal conflict, and this is often the reason for them 'giving in' to unreasonable demands on their time and energy, anything to avoid the inevitable unpleasantness if they do not.

Cannot Witness Violence Or Any Form Of Cruelty

Having to witness violence or any other form of cruelty can be extremely painful for the empath. They may show mimicry or emotional contagion

They will cover their eyes and ears, and experience high levels of anxiety. If reading a book, they will often cry, if watching a television series or a movie, they will show very strong visceral reactions and may get up and walk out to avoid being a witness.

As younger children, they will cry and run away if witnessing the schoolyard bully being mean and be traumatised by it.

Research has shown (36) that when giving subjects mild electrical shocks, individuals with high empathy levels will experience the same physical pain when watching it, and more so when it is a subject in a group they identify with.

Physical And Emotional Fatigue

Often suffer physical and emotional fatigue, can get weighed down by other's negative emotional energy so much so that it creates psychological disharmony.

Hangovers

They do not enjoy large crowds and can experience emotional and social hangovers. Introverts become overstimulated and exhausted a lot quicker than their counterparts.

Whilst they enjoy socialising as much as the average person, they approach it in a very different way, and will typically engage and talk to only a few people, but their conversations will be much deeper than banal small talk and gossiping. Empaths certainly do not lack the confidence to engage in social intercourse, and some actively seek out interesting debates on a wide range of topics, that will stimulate intellectual repartee and discourse.

It is in the pursuit of these deeper conversations that others will open up to the empath and share very personal and emotional stories with them, overloading them with negative and emotional baggage. Typically, the person they conversed with will feel much better after the conversation, as if they had a load lifted off their shoulders.

Sensory Overload

Empaths can easily become overwhelmed and overstimulated in noisy, crowded and busy areas due to Sensory Processing Sensitivity (SPS) and some may have Sensory Processing Disorder (SPD).

They may avoid big and loud gatherings, such as political rallies or music concerts, or any other noisy gathering. Even if they love music for example, and do attend a concert, they will feel the effects of sensory overload very quickly.

Sensory overload can be caused by a low threshold to stimulation from sound, light, smells, colours, touch (feeling crowded in) and incessant chatter or multiple conversations in the same room. When the five senses produce more inputs than the brain can handle and process at the same time, it may get 'stuck' trying to prioritise what to process first and will produce the symptoms of sensory overload.

Signs of sensory overload include:
- Extreme irritability
- Problems focusing due to competing inputs
- Discomfort and palpitations
- Restlessness and erratic movements
- Hyper-excitement and a feeling of being 'wound up' and off-balance

- Hyper-awareness of the environment and a feeling of needing to get out
- Stress, anxiety and even fear about your surroundings
- Closing your eyes, nose or even covering up your ears to stop the constant stream of inputs.
- Taking off items of clothing as they scratch or itch, even brushing or flossing your teeth hurts.
- Being revolted by anyone touching you, even if just a hand on your arm to calm you or stabilize you.
- Every sensory input is amplified into a cacophony of sounds, lights, smells, tastes and textures that becomes overwhelming and leaves you gasping for air.

Sensory overload builds up slowly but can quickly morph into a crescendo of sensual assaults if not dealt with timeously, by removing yourself from the situation and finding a calm place to recharge.

Linked To Social Anxiety

Empaths may be seen as suffering from social anxiety because they need to retreat and recharge so often, however, their motivation for shunning social contact for periods of time is very different to people with real social anxiety illness, which is mostly about fear of rejection as opposed to the empath's need to recharge their batteries so to speak in order to be available again for their social circle.

They can appear stand-offish or aloof, however, their aloofness is purely used as a protective device against inauthentic people. They can sense inauthenticity quicker than a dog can find a bone buried in the backyard, and once they have honed their personal protection skills, they will make an effort to avoid such people due to the chaos and problems they bring with them.

Isolated And Lonely

Empaths could become isolated and lonely, especially

if they give too much to close friend or intimate partner on an ongoing basis, which will leave them depleted, disoriented and less likely to socialise with a bigger circle of friends. They may also be deliberately isolated from family and friends by this person if there is underlying pathology.

Intimate Relationships

Empaths may become scared of intimate relationships and feel crowded very quickly. This is not based on fear of rejection as is commonly assumed, but rather on the overwhelming responsibility of taking on an intimate partner's happiness if there are no clear self-other boundaries in the relationship.

In addition, past mistakes in choosing an intimate partner, that turned out to be emotionally draining or abusive, may leave the empath with traces or scores of trust issues.

Often Need Time To Recharge

Empaths need time to recharge, often. This may conflict with busy schedules and daily demands on their time or other's expectations of their availability.

Other persons, whom may not know or understand the needs of the empath, may view this behaviour as erratic or being unreliable. They may see withdrawal periods as being anti-social, or depressed times. Inauthentic people will view their withdrawal from their incessant demands on their time and senses as being stuck-up or aloof.

However, if empaths do not recharge regularly, they will become overloaded, exhausted, confused and disoriented, and may start showing physical, emotional and psychological manifestations of long-term stress.

Selfish Friends

Because the empath is such a generous, loyal and caring friend, they open themselves up to being taken advantage of by the more selfish amongst their friends.

These spoiled, selfish individuals will quickly learn that the empath is always there for them, no matter time of day or whatever is going on in their own lives. They know, from experience, that the empath will drop whatever is happening at that moment to assist them, listen to them and empathise with their issues and problems.

Whilst it is the greatest gift to someone in real trouble, some friends will use their empath friend as a dumping ground for their emotional baggage and problems, acting as if it is their right to vent and dump whenever and oftentimes on a daily basis.

They leave the interaction feeling relieved of negative

energy, and validated, not even considering that the empath is holding all their negative energy and must try to make sense of it first before they can return to their own lives.

The friends are not malevolent, like energy vampires and dark triad personalities, they are just ignorant and selfish.

However, the constant dumping and emotional and psychological overload can leave the empath feeling drained, exhausted, depleted and may even present over the long term with depressive symptoms.

Emotional Vampires

Empaths and Highly Sensitive People (HSP's) easily fall victim to emotional vampires whom target them for their emotional strength.

It is a commonly used colloquial term for toxic

people, whom will drain the empath and leave them feeling completely exhausted. It was first termed by Albert Bernstein, Ph.D. in a book on the topic (35).

Whilst the term is often used to describe dark triad personalities, in this instance we are talking about toxic individuals that are simply self-absorbed, completely self-centred and whom will knowingly target others with warmth, compassion and healthy energy, to feed their own inner emptiness.

They include individuals that like to play the Victim, the Drama Queen, Constant Talkers (about themselves), the Antisocial (spurns social norms, reckless thrill seeker) and the Controlling personalities.

Emotional vampires lack three of the six pillars of self-esteem (35), as described by Mark Manson:
- Excessive need for validation or attention from others

- The belief that little to nothing is ever their fault
- The lack of self-awareness to recognize their self-defeating patterns

The danger here lies in the three traits reinforcing each other, and their ability to 'suck in and hurt good people' (36).

Emotional vampires are manipulative, jealous, lack empathy, have an excessive sense of entitlement and shows a blatant disregard for their effect on the empath's emotions.

They engage in extremely one-sided relationships, take whatever they can without blinking an eye, make decisions on your behalf without your consent and completely disregard your needs and wishes.

They create chaos wherever they go, will sabotage and undermine you at will, behave defensively and use projection extensively. It feels like they suck the air out of a room. Sadly, their negative influence can be felt long after they are gone.

Emotional vampires will dig at you with seemingly innocuous remarks (you're too sensitive) that eats away at your self-worth or deliver the jibe as a joke. The even more malignant dark triad personalities will make you seriously question your own worth.

They leave the empath feeling emotionally drained, exhausted, anxious, confused, frightened, emotionally unsafe, depressed and in pain. The empath may suddenly crave comfort foods and feel put down or dirtied.

They will affect the empath's ability to take care of themselves, their decision-making abilities as well as their physical, mental and emotional health.

Addictions

Sadly, empaths that have not learnt to take care of themselves may resort to addictions to numb their overloaded sensitivities, and engage in self-destructive behaviour such as overeating, alcohol, drugs and risky sexual endeavours.

Many empaths will overeat at times of stress or feeling threatened, in order to build up a symbolic protective layer around themselves.

Self-harming behaviour or attempted suicide is not common, but is possible, especially if there are underlying psychological and emotional issues.

Emotional Burnout

Emotional burnout occurs when an individual reaches a state of physical, mental and emotional exhaustion due to prolonged and ongoing stress. Initially, the term was used to describe emotional exhaustion in the health care professions, but it is now used for all stress related emotional exhaustion.

It leaves the individual feeling overwhelmed, completely drained emotionally and unable to meet demands made on them. They feel like they have nothing more to give, they are disengaged and detached, helpless, hopeless, defeated, cynical and very often extremely resentful. The overriding emotional exhaustion and cynicism are early tell-tale signs.

Eventually, emotional burnout will affect your ability to function and be a productive member of society and will cause long-term changes to your physical health.

Empaths that do not practice self-care are particularly vulnerable to emotional burnout, as are those in the midst of the emotional vortex that is a relationship with one of the dark triad personalities.

Whilst burnout is often the result of chronic and unrelenting stress, it is itself different from stress. Stress is always about 'too much' - too many physical, mental and emotional demands, whereas burnout is about 'not enough' – feeling emotionally drained and blunted, without motivation, mentally exhausted and dried up, feeling completely empty with nothing left to give.

The most commonly used burnout questionnaire is the Maslach Burnout Inventory Scale, administered by psychologists. (38) It measures subscales called Emotional Exhaustion, Depersonalisation, Cynicism, Personal Accomplishment and Involvement. If the first three measures high and the last two low, it points to burnout.

Narcissists And Other Dark Triad Personalities

Empaths are often targeted by dark triad personalities because of their giving natures and big hearts and may end up being severely abused, emotionally, mentally, physically, financially and sexually. They may even be induced into a life of crime on behalf of the abuser, even though they have no criminal inclinations themselves.

What are the dark triad personalities?

The dark triad (DT) traits include:

- Narcissism
- Machiavellianism
- Psychopathy

It is referred to as 'dark' because of their extremely malevolent qualities, and individuals with these traits are more likely to commit crimes. They cause social distress and leave chaos in their wake wherever they go. They often manipulate their way into leadership positions and can decimate organisations or even countries.

They have been linked, collectively, to deficits in empathy and increased aggression, however, the specific links are being examined in many different research programs. It is not clear if the lack of empathy is the dark core that drives indirect aggression, or if it is specific empathic trait deficits that are slightly different in each.

One recent study showed Narcissism to be differentiated from the other two in that there were higher levels of cognitive empathy, whereas they showed a greater lack of cognitive empathy of the affect (39).

Dark triad personalities are truly malignant 'energy vampires' and will deliberately target their victims without remorse. Although they are distinct traits there is a lot of overlap, and all three are associated with a callous-manipulative interpersonal style (40). They are considered the three personality variables that contribute the most to aversive social behaviour.

They score low on Agreeableness and Conscientiousness in the Big 5, but some show Neuroticism. Some dark triad personalities, however, do show Altruism, but only when it is perceived that the altruism would benefit them personally (41).

Narcissism

This trait is characterised by:

- egotism
- pride
- grandiosity
- dominance
- lack of affective empathy
- unwilling or unable to identify with other's feelings
- high on Extraversion and Openness

Malignant narcissism, a particularly severe form,

presents with:

- grandiose narcissism
- paranoia
- sadism
- anti-social behaviours
- lack of moral reasoning
- aggression

Machiavellianism

Characterised by:

- focus on self-interest
- deception
- manipulation of others
- exploitation
- lack of morality (cynical disregard for)
- unprincipled
- cold
- suspicious
- low on Agreeableness and Conscientiousness

Psychopathy

The most malevolent of the dark triad personalities, and characterised by severe:

- selfishness
- impulsivity
- thrill-seeking
- antisocial behaviour
- callousness
- lack of remorse
- lack of cognitive empathy for affect
- not distress by the suffering of victims
- low on Agreeableness, Conscientiousness and Neuroticism (secondary psychopathy can score high on Neuroticism)

Main characteristics of the Dark Triad personality traits Source: D'Souza (2016). (42)

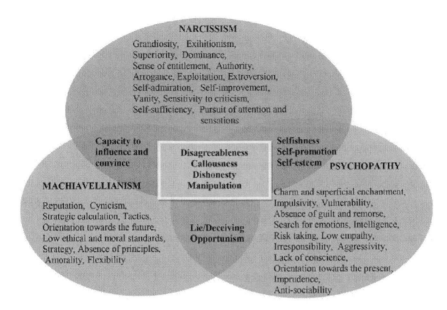

Why do they target empaths?

Manipulative personalities such as the dark triad personalities will see a source of energy – a 'free ride' so to speak, in empaths and HSP's.

They see a:

- loving, caring person
- full of warmth, giving generously
- will take care of them

- be devoted to them
- listen to what they say
- do what they are asked to do

They will also target anyone that appears to be:

- lonely, hurt
- low on self-esteem
- in need of a savior

They will present a false self, quite deliberately:

- charming
- intelligent
- giving
- caring
- interested in everything you are interested in
- invent a reason for you to take care of them emotionally (i.e. family rejection, divorce, lost child, the list of fake hurts is endless)

They will pick a target:

- very deliberately
- find out as much as they can about them before introducing themselves (even to the point of stalking) if possible
- fake openness and trustworthiness
- encourage you to share your deep secrets (and this is very seductive to the empath whom always get dumped with other's emotions and secrets)
- pledge to take care of you and protect you
- pathologically lie to impress you
- hint at their deep pain and need for healing to reel you in

Once the empath has taken the bait and is now connected to the manipulator, they will

- engage in confusing behavior
- getting angry about minor things
- then claiming it was just stress
- or you misunderstood

- or they did not get angry (gas lighting) it is your imagination
- promise never to do it again
- blame it on an abusive childhood

This behaviour gradually escalates over time, but the moment you do not do things in their way, they will:

- be cold
- punishing
- withholding
- emotionally abusive
- verbally abusive with jibes, dismissed as jokes
- recruiting your friends and family against you (triangulation)
- breaking down your sense of self
- making you mistrust your own judgment.

Often it becomes an abusive relationship in the extreme

- isolation – making sure you do not socialize or see your family or friends
- financially – withholding financial support and even controlling your money and resources
- sexually – demanding sexual intimacy whenever their needs dictate, irrespective of your feelings
- psychologically – breaking down your sense of self, gaslighting, triangulating
- emotionally – calling you hypersensitive and paranoid, sometimes even delusional
- physically – intimidation with threats of leaving, threats of violence or killing you or your family, and actual physical violence.

Empaths and Narcissists can create the 'Perfect Storm' of destructive relationships – the empath wants to heal the narcissist, whom callously just want to suck them dry emotionally, use up all their resources for his own benefit and leave them in chaos and destruction.

Hsps (Highly Sensitive Persons)

About 15 to 20% of people have a psychological trait that is known as Sensory Processing Sensitivity (SPS) (35). This is not the same as the disorder known as Sensory Processing Disorder, but there are similar signs and symptoms.

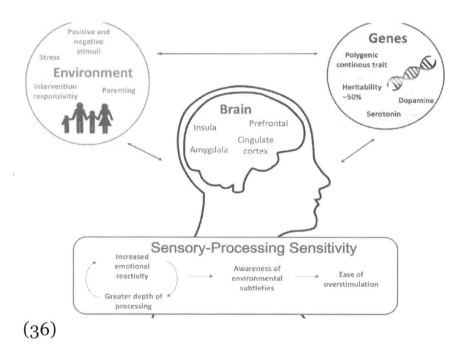

(36)

Highly Sensitive Persons (HSP) (34) has been

recognized as a personality trait.

HSP's show signs of extreme sensitivity to emotions, crowds, light, sound, and touch. Recent research has concentrated on the theory of differential susceptibility to the environment. (35) They do not, however, absorb the emotions and energy from other people, the way empaths do.

They are often called shy or timid, even introverted, but a large portion of HSP's are actually extroverted. They are unusually creative and often intellectually gifted.

Medics, Medications And Misdiagnoses

Extreme mood swings and unaccounted for sadness and depression may lead an empath, whom has not yet learned the reasons for them picking up so many diverse emotions in a short time, and whom does not have a clear self-them understanding, to think there is something wrong.

Overworked and inattentive medical staff may misdiagnose an empath as having social anxiety, bipolar disorder illness or borderline personality disorder.

There are however differences that we need to understand.

Social Anxiety

Many people experience mild forms of social anxiety when in a new social situation or having to present a talk or paper in a public forum, and introverts or shy people may just simply not enjoy big crowds or new people.

With social anxiety though, these normal social situations make them so uncomfortable and cause such extreme stress that they avoid it at all cost.

Social anxiety or phobia is a mental condition, presenting as 'an intense and very persistent fear of being watched or judged by others' (36). It interferes with everyday activities such as school, work and other social situations, making it very hard to keep friends. They are intensely afraid of humiliation, being judged or rejected.

In social situations they will display symptoms of anxiety, such as sweating, rapid heartbeat, nausea, rigid body posture, averting eyes, speaking very softly, and often blanking out. They will avoid social contact as much as possible.

Differences between social anxiety and the empath:
- People with social anxiety are not naturally drawn to others, children or animals.
- People are not comfortable talking to them nor spilling their secrets and anxieties to them

- They do not easily make friends like an empath does.
- Their avoidance of crowds or groups of people is constant and ongoing and grounded in fear of humiliation and rejection.
- This is quite unlike the empath that needs to recharge in quiet and may from time to time avoid others to protect themselves from overload.

Bipolar

As empaths may experience wild emotional swings during a day, due to them absorbing the emotions and energy surrounding them, they may appear to be mentally and emotionally unstable to the uninformed. If they are not aware of the implications of their empathic traits, they may seek medical input and may be misdiagnosed as being bipolar.

Bipolar Disorder is a mental health condition, also known as manic depression that causes unusual and extreme mood swings. Mania or hypomania presents as euphoric feelings, feeling very energetic or incredibly irritable. In the depression phase, the person feels sad, low, blue, hopeless and loses interest in most pleasurable activities. Episodes may occur rarely or often and can last anything from days to weeks to months (36).

It affects sleep, activity and judgment and often leads to irrational and illogical thought patterns and behavior, and reality distortions.

The extreme highs and lows differ from person to person, and the disease affects everyone differently. Both bipolar disorder and empaths display extreme emotions, however, there are huge differences in the source and type and duration of emotions. Cognitive empathy is low in Bipolar disorder (45).

Main Differences

- A Bipolar sufferer can become reckless or out of control during a manic episode.
- Empaths are much more in control of their emotions and will withdraw if they become overwhelmed.
- During bipolar manic episodes, the episodes last much longer, even days, whereas the mood swings of the empath are much shorter and related to the energy they absorb from the people and the environment surrounding them at the time.
- Bipolar disorder sufferers are much less likely to display empathy towards others, whereas empaths have very high levels of empathy.

Bpd

Borderline Personality Disorder is a mental disorder characterised by the person displaying 'an ongoing pattern of varying moods, self-image, and behaviour.' (37)

It is characterized by extensive behavioural and interpersonal problems related to cognitive and emotional dysfunction, and they have low cognitive empathy (46). This manifests as mood swings, intense episodes of depression, anxiety and anger that can last from a few hours to days. They are uncertain of self and their role in the world so can change values, interests and opinions at breakneck speed.

They see the world in black and white and can switch on friends and loved ones in a heartbeat, swinging from idealisation to devaluation, which leads to incredibly intense and unstable relationships.

They suffer chronic feelings of emptiness, a distorted self-image, dissociation and often partake in dangerous and reckless behaviours such as binge eating, alcohol or drug abuse, unsafe sex, spending sprees, and reckless driving. They demonstrate highly impulsive behaviours. They also show an abnormal fear of abandonment.

Differences Between Bpd And The Empath

- Empaths never experience feelings of emptiness
- They do not fear abandonment, but rather the opposite of being swallowed up in a relationship when their self-other distinction is not well developed.
- They may share mood swings, but the nature of the mood swings is different, an empath's sadness lasts as long as the person they picked up the sadness from.
- They may both resort to unsafe behaviours, however, the BPD does it to fill an ever-present gaping hole and the empath tries to numb themselves from an overload of input.
- Empaths remain loyal and caring and always has a big heart.

Of course, an empath may have an underlying mental

problem, but those cases are far and few between.

Protecting Yourself

Learn How To Protect Yourself As An Empath

Whilst the wonderful positive gifts of the empath can greatly enrich the individual's life, it is important to learn how to use these gifts appropriately so as to protect yourself.

The dark side of being an empath can be a real threat to your physical, mental, emotional and social health, and it is a slippery slope to emotional burnout, or worse, being trapped in abusive relationships, if you do not establish a firm sense of self, boundaries and accommodations for your sensitivities and emotions.

If you find yourself with symptoms of:

- Fuzzy thinking
- short temper
- droopy eyelids
- feelings of guilt
- emotional exhaustion,

- fueling with caffeine, or
- drinking more alcohol than usual

It is definitely time to sit back and reassess and find a way back to yourself.

But how do you protect yourself against this in the first place?

How do you lead a rich and fulfilling life without constantly having to be on your guard?

What steps can you put in place to ensure you don't fall victim to emotional and sensory overload?

Strategies For Handling The Challenges Of Feeling And Absorbing So Many Stimuli

Broad strategies and common advice dished out to empaths on how to handle the challenges of feeling so much, or absorbing so many stimuli, typically include one or more of the following:

- Learn how to embrace your gift of feeling so deeply or how to recognize your own emotions.
- Manage stress
- Exercise regularly, sleep well
- Confide in your friends
- Talk to a therapist
- Remember the temporary nature of feeling overwhelmed, i.e. this too shall pass
- Tell people in your work or social circles that you become overwhelmed in noisy environments
- Explain that retreating to a quiet place will help
- Practice self-compassion, refrain from criticizing yourself.

The Four R's

Building a strategy to protect yourself for the long haul requires a comprehensive plan, with clear to-dos and long-term goals.

A good place to start this strategy is to draw a map, outline the overall goals, and the broad steps to take to achieve them, as well as practical hands-on advice on how to implement the plan.

The three R's model (recognize – reverse – resilience) is often used as a starting point by psychologists, however, it may be prudent to take a step back, to start at the beginning with setting clear goals, namely reevaluating your priorities. What is it that you would like to see in the long term? Where do you want to be? How do you want to feel and act?

Thus, the Four R's (53):
- Reevaluate
- Recognize
- Resilience
- Reverse

Let us look at each in turn.

Reevaluate Priorities

Decide if you want to live your life proactively, leading to a rich and fulfilling existence, or if you are satisfied to be dragged from episode to episode of emotional exhaustion and eventually burnout, trying to survive and maybe hiding out as much as possible to avoid any further overload.

- Commit to loving yourself enough to engage actively in self-care.
- Commit to understanding your gifts and the potential problems so as to build a strong resistance.
- Commit to building resilience so as to bounce back no matter what life throws at you.

Whilst most people will claim that their priorities are very important to them, very few could list them, nor rank them. Even less will make the time to ensure that they are aligning their daily actions to their priorities.

The late Steven Covey, in his pioneering book 'The 7 Habits of Highly Effective People', presented the world with a simple framework for evolving into a highly effective person. Whilst it was snapped up by the business community as a 'how to manage your time better' guideline, its truly enduring messages are that

- change starts from within,
- you must begin with the end in mind, and the most profound
- Put First Things First.

This is what reevaluating your priorities and giving depth and meaning to your life, are all about.

Remember the story of the teacher that gave her class items to put in a glass jar? They started with a layer of sand, then a layer of gravel, then small stones, and finally big stones. However by this time, the jar was full, and there was no space for the bigger stones.

She then taught the class to see

- the stones as the most important things in our lives, for example, our health, our family, things we cannot live without. And to always put first things first.
- The small stones represent the things that matter to you a great deal, but that you can live without – so if you only had big stones, your life would still be full, as they are not essential to your wellbeing.
- The gravel represents the 'nice-to-have' things in your life, a well-deserved vacation, a spa treatment, a special set of books. Things that make life fun and exciting, but not essential in the real sense of the word.
- The sand represents the fillers, the things that you do because you feel obliged to but that does not bring you any joy, or the useless things we

buy because it is on sale or someone else has one and loves it.

If you put the big stones in first, then the smaller ones, then the gravel, and lastly the least important, the sand, there is often room for it all – but that is not really the point, you need to clarify what are the things to put first.

If you constantly fill your glass with sand and gravel, you will never have space for the most important things in your life.

This 'rock, pebble and sand' analogy is also often used as a time management training tool. However, we are not talking about time management per se, we are talking about your emotional and mental wellbeing, which is much more important.

But, where do you start?

Steps To Take Action

Write them down

If you have never done this before, it may take a few days or even weeks to get them into a format that will be easy to remember or that makes sense to you.

Start by jotting down a few notes – anywhere that works for you, on a notepad, or in your Notes on your smartphone, or a journal. Go back to your list every day and add to it, or make changes, or clarify what you meant.

It needs to make sense to you, you do not have to put down lofty ideals that you think someone else wants to see, or that will make you look good. Be honest, what really matters to you. You can play a game with yourself, for instance, if you had to pick three to five things that you cannot or do not want to give up, ever, what would it be? Play this with your friends, it may help you clarify your priorities.

Rank Your Priorities

Once you have a consolidated list, rank them in order of importance. It will help you clarify your needs and be a constant reminder to spend your time and energy where it matters most.

Turn Them Into Actions

A list of priorities is not of much use unless you can translate them to your daily life. Turn them into something you can do – for each priority list a number of action steps.

For example, if 'family' was one of your priorities, some action steps may be 'gadget-free family meals' or 'read a story to my child every night'.

Review

The old adage 'you cannot manage what you cannot measure' applies here too. It does not mean measuring activity as you would at work, but you do need to monitor yourself, and see where you are sticking to your commitments and priorities and what is slipping. And slipping is almost guaranteed, life happens, no matter the most carefully laid plans.

Regular reviewing and monitoring of your priorities will help you keep on track, remind you of what is really important in life, and help you not 'sweat the small stuff'.

For the empath, this means having to really focus on yourself, your loved ones and your long-term goals, and not being sidetracked and hooked by your need to help others, which often leads to the exclusion of your family and your own emotional health.

Maybe posting them on your bathroom mirror, or

your fridge, or the side of your computer screen, or even turning a shot of them into the wallpaper on your smartphone, will ensure that you see them on a regular basis, and help you keep on track.

Action Expresses Priorities.

If you neglect your priorities, your life is likely to become unstable. Clarifying your priorities is about building a strong foundation for yourself like you would if you built a house.

Building a strong foundation includes making self-care a priority for the empath. But how do you build self-care into your life?

Self-Care

Self-care is not a luxury we get to indulge in every now and then. It is about your respecting yourself enough to care for your overall health.

Living a healthier, fulfilling life is about creating balance in all spheres of health.

Everything Is Connected

Compartmentalization may work as a strategy for very short periods of time but can be very damaging. Your mental, emotional, social, spiritual, financial, and physical health are all interconnected, and as is your environment and lifestyle choices

Eliminate Stress

A reasonable amount of stress can motivate you to do what needs to be done, however persistent, long-term stress can wreak havoc with your life and health. Either make serious efforts to change the situation or remove yourself from the situation.

Live In The Moment

Longing for the 'good old days' or thinking if only I had 'x' will definitely make you miserable and have you losing out on life. Enjoy every moment. You can control how you react to what is happening right now.

Appreciate What You Have

Focus on the positives in your life and stop trying to compete with the Joneses.

Take A Long-Term View On Health

This means getting vaccinated as required, avoiding polluted areas, doing your required check-ups when necessary and being cognizant of any genetic-based risks in health and what steps you need to take to protect yourself.

Live A Healthful Life

Chasing every latest fad on the internet is one of the

worst things you can possibly do. Follow the science, read up on healthy living at verified scientific sites, for example, Mayo Clinic, Harvard, AHA, etc.

Get Moving!

It does not really matter how, do whatever you enjoy and that does not cause pain or discomfort. Moving at least once an hour during the day brings untold health benefits.

Exercise

- reduces stress,
- increases energy and
- produces feel-good hormones.

Make Every Meal A Feast!

Feasting is not just for special occasions, a treat, or a guilty pleasure. Prepare healthy balanced meals as a feast to look forward to and enjoy every sensuous bite. Include proteins, lots of fruit, vegetables, and healthy grains. Enjoy your glass of wine or cup of coffee.

Avoid Any Form Of Substance Abuse

Find a way to quit smoking, and if you have any other substance abuse problems, get help.

Hydrate

Drinking enough water or eating fruits and food with high water content such as orange or cucumber slices helps

- keep you hydrated throughout the day,
- minimizes the load on the heart,
- assists muscle and joint movement,
- removes waste and
- maintains your temperature.

Sleep

Getting enough quality sleep is important for

- healing damaged cells,
- boosting your immune system,
- stabilizing weight hormones,
- recharging the cardiovascular system.
- helps with learning through a process called memory consolidation.

Sleep deprivation leads to:

- irritability,
- moodiness and a
- greater risk for accidents.

Take Breaks

Self-care includes taking regular breaks to revitalize. It includes small and longer breaks, and the benefits include

- increased productivity and creativity,

- memory consolidation and improved learning,
- restore motivation and
- decrease decision fatigue.

Prioritize Your Close Relationships

Investing in what is most important in the long term, by giving your full attention to your closest relationship, will bring feelings of self-worth, satisfaction and warmth. Enjoy, have fun and be all there.

Socialize

Quit being so serious and have some fun with your social groups. Regular social contact and connecting are more important to health than diet and exercise.

Believe In Something

Spirituality and religious belief are beneficial to longevity. It may be something as simple as believing in kindness or paying-it-forward. Finding meaning in any form can benefit your health and others.

Show Gratitude

Practicing gratitude helps you focus on the positive, and leads to

- increased levels of well-being,
- self-control,
- optimism and
- happiness.
- It helps strengthen interpersonal relationships.

Recognise

Learn To Recognise Your Own Feelings

Once you become more self-aware you will be able to pick up on your own feelings and recognise symptoms of discomfort or overload.

Distinguish Between Emotions You Carry On Behalf Of Another Person And Your Own Emotions

This may be a little bit harder, when you absorb so much emotional distress and energy from others the line between what you are feeling and what they were feeling can become a little bit blurred.

Think about how you felt before you started engaging with this particular person,

- What was your mood like? What did they talk about during the interaction?
- What was their mood like during the interaction?
- Did they feel better, calmer, more centered after the interaction?
- Did you pick up their bad mood, or emotional distress, frustration or anger during the conversation or visit?
- Is this the first time this happened with this person or do you frequently pick up their emotional distress to your own detriment?

Don t Fight Negative Feelings

Don't try to make yourself feel better by masking negative feelings.

If you have picked up another individual's distress and negative energy, admit that it is not yours, and distance yourself from it.

If you are feeling sad or hurt, frustrated or angry, identify the emotion, the cause of it, and determine if it is something you can fix or not.

If not accept the feeling as part of your growth, and work through it.

Stay In The Present

Understand that all feelings have a transient nature, and that recognising the feeling, and choosing to move forward will help you to eventually lift your mood

Do not engage in morbid rumination about the interaction, or previous acts or omissions, and how things could be different 'if only' you did something differently.

Do not engage in wishful thinking about how you will retaliate or do better in future or how things could be different 'if only' you had something else.

Stay in the present, feel your feelings but give yourself a time-limit before moving on.

Resilience

Empaths are often told 'you are hypersensitive' or 'you need to develop a thicker skin', which can be very unfair and hurtful.

One of the most critical strategies for protecting yourself is to build resilience.

What Is Resilience?

Resilience is the ability to recover quickly from difficulties, to bounce back so to speak. It hints at toughness, like the ability of an object to spring back into shape.

Some people cave under adversity, responding with a flood of emotions and a very strong sense of uncertainty and confusion. Those with strong resilience, that cultivate their skills are able to not only mitigate the effects of adverse events but can adapt to them and return to normal functioning or even better, thriving, relatively quickly.

Resilience is 'that ineffable quality that allows some people to be knocked down by life and come back at least as strong as before' (53)

It does not mean that they do not experience pain and sadness or distress, the road to resilience is paved with considerable emotion and distress. However, it involves thoughts, actions and behaviors that can be learnt.

Resilience Factors

According to the American Psychological Association (APA), factors that contribute to resilience include:

- Caring and supportive relationships (family and other) that
- Create trust and love
- Provide role models
- Offer encouragement
- Reassurance
- A Positive view of self
- Confidence in your strengths and abilities
- Capacity to make realistic plans
- Take steps to carry out those plans

- Capacity to manage your impulses
- Manage strong feelings

When you have resilience, you can access or harness that inner strength to help you cope when adversity strikes.

When you lack resilience, you may feel victimized, ruminate, become overwhelmed or turn to unhealthy coping mechanisms such as overeating or substance abuse.

Resilience gives you the ability to see past current problems, deal with stress and find fulfillment and enjoyment. It protects against mental problems and improves your ability to cope.

The psychological resources required to cushion the deleterious effects of stress or suffering makes up the essence of Resilience:

- Strong self-esteem,
- Optimism,
- Mastery of your emotions,
- Ability to see failure as feedback

Optimism can blunt the impact of the adverse events on the mind and body. This allows access to cognitive resources to evaluate what happened and how different behavioural paths could have generated more productive outcomes, in a cool and objective manner.

How To Build Resilience For The Empath

Know yourself and limits

Be clear on your goals and what you can or cannot handle. This means that you do not have to push past your own limits if it affects your mental and emotional health.

Advice can be confusing, yes you need to stretch

yourself, but in a positive way, doing new things that excite you and enriches your life.

Accepting behaviour and inputs from others that pushes way past your limits of emotional inputs will damage your inner peace, disorient and confuse you and leave you emotionally drained.

Learn to recognise when you have had enough, and walk away, maybe for a few minutes to regroup, or for good. Be firm and consistent with your limits and draw a line in the sand.

If you tell a loved one or friend that they are crossing a line, expect them to respect that line, every time. If you draw a line one day, and the next time they cross it, you allow that to happen, maybe because you are too exhausted to point it out, or you just cannot be bothered as nothing changes, nothing will change. They will continue to cross your lines because you allow it.

Strengthen your sense of me-them

Do not get lost in blurred lines between your feelings and that of others.

Theory of Mind is a very important social-cognitive skill that develops over time in young children, where we learn to think about your own and other's mental states, and helps you understand that other people may think differently to yourself.

So in essence, what we think is going on in someone else's mind is just our theory. For the empath, whom feel other's emotions and absorb them like a sponge would water, it is important to strengthen the theory of mind, to understand, at a cognitive level, that you may sense the other person's feelings, but you do not fully comprehend what they are thinking.

Thus, if you sense sadness, it does not mean that they

would experience sadness the way you would, or be sad for the same reasons. You need to identify, if for instance you suddenly feel sad in another's presence, whose feeling it really is, yours or theirs? This takes practice in real life and can be hard to overcome, but it is a strong building block in strengthening your sense of self and building your resilience.

Notice your suffering

Be ruthless with naming your suffering for what it is, giving too much, feeling too much, this way you can learn to say no when you need to.

Empaths often suffer in silence, in order to help others, and can do immeasurable harm to their own mental health by not acknowledging nor naming their suffering.

Putting it out there, verbally, makes it real, takes it out the closet, and opens the path for you to learn to set boundaries and say no to protect yourself.

Practice self-compassion

Give yourself a break and accept that change is part of life and a mistake is just another opportunity to learn.

Be kind to yourself at all times. Allow yourself the compassion you so generously dole out to others.

You can have an empathic conversation with yourself in the mirror – it will help you see how hard you are on yourself.

Learn to control your emotions

Which might be really hard to do, especially for the emotional empath - you have to practice this all the time.

If you allow your emotions to get the better of you,

you hand over your power. Emotional reactions blur your ability to think logically and make proper decisions. You end up splashing and drowning in a pool of negativity and emotions.

If a child accidentally fell into a pool you would tell him to stay calm, tread water and stop thrashing, so you can talk him to the edge of the pool or get in to go get him. Controlling your emotions works in exactly the same way. Take a deep breath, don't lash out, tell yourself this is not the end of the world, regroup and find something to distract you until you can think more clearly.

Some people count to ten, others have found help by using the anxiety-busting coping mechanism to identify

- Five things you see around you
- Four things you can touch around you
- Three things you hear
- Two things you can smell

- One thing you can taste

Concentrate on maintaining calmness.

Control your reactions

To other's comments, actions or omissions and emotions. You cannot stop how you feel in the moment, but you can learn to control your reaction to that feeling, that is where your real power lies.

When you feel yourself wanting to jump in and fix things, or tell them what to do, or what you really think, or what the actual truth is, stop yourself.

Take a moment to breathe in and out a few times and try to clarify your feeling. Then make an attempt to be logical about what was said or what happened, and only respond when you are ready to do so calmly.

For the empath, the major obstacle to overcome in

controlling their reactions is to stop taking the bait hook line and sinker.

Do not jump in to come to the rescue all the time. Sit back and let the person talk and give him space to try figure it out for himself.

In most cases if he is not able to figure out a solution himself, it is because he does not want to solve the problem, he is simply manipulating you to do his bidding and disguising it as an emotional conundrum.

Accept that you cannot help every person you meet.

Keep Perspective

Stop seeing every setback as an insurmountable problem, learn to control how you interpret and respond to these events.

Learn to distinguish between an event, your life and yourself as a person of substance.

Take criticism grain of salt, and consider the source.

Make Connections

Build meaningful and deep relationships

- with family and friends,
- join social groups, faith-based or spiritual organizations or
- find volunteer opportunities.

Asking for and accepting support and connection (circling the wagons) is a big factor in building resilience.

Evaluate your close friends

Take a good look at your close friends and your intimate social circle.

Do they provide you with love, laughter, support, positivity, and uplifting experiences?

Do you look forward to seeing them or do you feel dread when they call to meet up?

Do they talk about interesting events or activities that you and others in your circle may be interested in, or do they only talk about themselves and their achievements or problems?

Are you able to have deep and meaningful conversations with them above life, or do they shy away from anything that is not superficial?

Do they respect others, their parents, their family, their colleagues, and friends and try to lift them up, or do they spend their time gossiping about others and breaking them down? Do they think denigrating others, especially their parents, make them cool?

Are you comfortable sharing deep feelings or secrets with them, or do you wonder if you can trust them with something so personal?

Are you comfortable asking them for support and understanding when you need it, or do you feel they may belittle you or attack you if you show any perceived weakness?

Do they accept you with all your idiosyncrasies or do they constantly tell you to do better or how to change yourself?

Do they respect your boundaries or do they expect you to do their bidding and get angry or withdraw if you do not comply with their requirements?

If there is nothing but negativity let them go or they

will drag you down

Ignore your inner critic

You need to stop criticizing yourself and give up on perfectionism – it is time to slay the dragons and live in the present.

Everyone has insecurities and fears, maybe a bad memory or two that nags at them day in and day out. It is the individual that can convince themselves that whatever went wrong is now firmly in the past and that every mistake or put down is an opportunity to learn.

strong self-esteem and sense of self will also help you see that whatever was or is said to you is just another's opinion and does not necessarily constitute the truth.

Einstein is famously quoted for saying ,'everyone is a

genius, but if you judge a fish by its ability to climb a tree, it will live its whole life believing that it is stupid'.

Whilst there is no evidence that he actually said this, it holds universal truths in that we all have different skills and abilities and we have our own innate genius – it is absurd to judge everyone according to one standard, especially yourself, but it also points to the issue of self-belief, it is equally absurd to spend your life believing you are stupid because someone else said you are.

Set Healthy Boundaries

Everything in life is interlinked and setting healthy boundaries is part of building self-esteem and resilience

- communicate how you feel openly and honestly,
- take responsibility for your own happiness,
- follow through on what you say,
- expect your boundaries to be respected,

- take responsibility for your own actions
- never assume or guess the other person's feelings
- know and accept when you need to move on.

Nurture a positive self-image

See yourself as

- strong and rational,
- able to solve problems,
- trust your instincts and
- do not allow yourself being preyed on

Set Realistic Goals

Clarify your goals, write them down and then purposefully pursue them.

Make sure they are your goals and not those of your loved ones or friends.

Small victories will strengthen your resolve and resilience.

Reclaim your power and pursue your own dreams.

It may be as simple as making time for half an hour of practicing a hobby you enjoy after you have put the kids to bed, or as grand and far-reaching as you can imagine.

Make your day Meaningful

Do things you enjoy and will give you a sense of purpose and meaning

At the end of each day, you need to be able to look at at least a few things that you really enjoyed, and that you are grateful for.

Make a habit of reviewing the day in a few minutes of quiet time before bed, put aside the things that went wrong to deal with later, and be grateful for what you enjoyed.

Be Proactive

Don't ignore problems by playing ostrich and hiding your head in the sand, if you suspect something may happen or go wrong.

Figure out what needs to be done to Prevent it, fix it, or mitigate the effects if it cannot be fixed.

Then make a plan of action and implement it.

Get professional help

If you feel that you are not making progress building resilience, or if you do not know where to start, approach a professional for assistance. It is imperative for your mental well-being, and time and money well spent.

How To Limit Inputs During Interactions With Others

- **Reflect their feelings back to them**

To ensure that you do not take on everyone else's emotional garbage, learn how to reflect their feelings back to them

- **Allow venting for specific amounts of time only**

If you have friends or colleagues or intimate partners that are always upset and living from one drama to the next, set limits to the amount of time they are allowed to vent per encounter. If they are frustrated or angry or upset with a specific situation, limit the length of time they can vent for (say six months for the loss of a partner) before they have to move on and

- **Learn to say 'Not my monkey'**

Every time you find yourself engaging in someone else's affairs or frustrations, remind yourself what is really important for you to deal with, and what the other person's own responsibilities are.

- **Commit to 'No more walking on eggshells'**

If someone makes you so uncomfortable that you feel like you have to tiptoe around them or 'walk on eggshells' it is time to set very strong boundaries or move on

- **Negotiate a compromise**

With that very obsessive-compulsive person in your life – whom wants everything done just so according to their requirements. Tell them what you can and cannot commit to and negotiate a compromise that will suit both of you.

- **Reclaim your power**

By pursuing your own goals, dreams and friendships rather than just follow those of other people in your life. Try out new things you have always wanted to do, go out and make new friends that will enhance your life

- **Detox from toxic people**

By taking time for yourself to recharge and restore your energy levels even if it is just a short break

- **Shielding**

In the moment is a good strategy if you start to feel overwhelmed, however, it is not a sustainable long-term coping mechanism. Shielding involves visualizing yourself building an imaginary shield around you to protect you from the onslaught of inputs (like a bubble that cannot be penetrated)

- **Spend some time in nature**

Go for a walk, or plan a hiking holiday, spend some time on the beach, walk barefoot on the lawn, do some gardening or play with your dog.

- **Practice Mindfulness**

This means becoming aware of the actual moment you are in. Mastering mindfulness takes practice and getting some assistance can help you to use it to ground yourself even during interactions to help you control your emotions.

Emotional Vampires And Dark Triad Traits

Malevolent and non-malevolent Emotional Vampires can wreak havoc with an Empath's emotions and sanity. Specific tactics to deal with emotional vampires include:

- **Get support** from your friends (circle the wagons) by opening up and explaining to them what you are dealing with and ask for help.
- **Get to know the enemy** and how they operate. Learn about the different types of emotional vampires and the tactics they employ to hook you.
- Identify and learn what **your particular hooks** are, and look out for them when meeting new people, or dealing with people currently in your life.
- **Know who you are dealing with**, do not underestimate the chaos and damage an emotional vampire can leave in their wake. Be brave and concede that you may have been fooled by a very experienced trickster.
- **Avoid making hasty decisions** about anything related to the emotional vampire, and do not cave to pressure if you are uncomfortable with any interaction with them

- Emotional vampires can be very **predictable**, making your escape easier
- **Get the upper hand** by observing them from multiple angles, enlist the help of friends to help clarify their tactics and manipulations
- **Learn to walk away** from emotional vampires for good, sometimes going NO contact is the only way forward and cutting the cord becomes essential for your emotional freedom
- **Don't try to reason** with an emotional vampire, it is a complete waste of time, as they are not interested in reason but only their own agenda, rather use your mental resources for selfcare
- Emotional vampires are **deeply unhappy** people, they are insecure and weak and will show no goodwill, so do not make excuses for them or try and cover for them
- **Avoid their emotions** at all cost, lest it infects your mood, if you cannot separate yourself from the person (i.e. your boss or family member)

- **If they show rage**, keep your distance as far as possible, show a poker face, be very stoic, and show them that their emotions do not affect yours.
- **If they start an argument**, do not get others dragged in and avoid taking sides at all costs.
- **Do not fall prey to their manipulations**, be on the lookout for them and stick to your resolve to deal with them in a mature and calm manner.
- **You can show compassion** but set limits on the emotional diplomacy you display; this will free you from their hold over you and reduce the emotional drain
- **Clarify your relationships** with anyone showing emotional vampire traits, and walk away if your circumstances allow; if it affects you too severely walk away anyway and deal with the consequences as they may arise.
- **Focus intently** when you deal with an emotional vampire, remind yourself constantly that your aim is not rehabilitation, some people

cannot be 'saved', but counter them with common grace

Specific tips for dealing with the:

Narcissist

- Set realistic expectations, and remind yourself they won't change
- Ensure that your self-worth is not dependent on the other person
- Do not confide your deepest feelings or divulge any secrets as they will use it against you
- If contact is unavoidable your best tactic is to engage in the tedious ego stroking, they crave without getting emotionally involved
- However, the best strategy is no contact

Victim

- Set kind but very firm limits
- Do not pander to their pity party
- Listen briefly then ask for solutions

- Use your body language to enforce limits you have set
- Do not offer to solve their problems, even if it is the quickest way to get them away from you
- If they behave in a paranoid way, empathize with their emotions but do not engage in facts
- Show them clearly that you are not condoning their behavior
- Keep your distance

Controller

- Be assertive and calm
- Never try to control a controller, it will not end well
- Don't tell them what to do and do not consult with them
- Explain that you appreciate their opinion, but that you need to do this yourself
- If an intervention is required, change the subject, or try to get them into a group of people to diffuse the moment

Constant talker

- They do not respond to nonverbal clues so you will have to speak up and interrupt them, no matter how tough it may be for you to do so
- If you need an escape, claim a prior appointment and leave or show them the door.
- Do not indulge them in any way

Drama queen

- Remember they can't draw energy from equanimity, so stay calm and take deep breaths
- Count silently in your head to restore or maintain your mental equilibrium
- Know your priorities and concentrate on that
- Do not get yourself caught up in their histrionics or try to offer advice or help
- Set limits and stick to them

Reverse - How To Recharge When You Get Over-Cooked '

Remember that

- a strong self-esteem,
- optimism,
- mastery of your emotions and
- the ability to learn from mistakes

constitute the psychological resources to buffer you from the deleterious effects of stress and emotional overload.

Whilst making self-care the foundation of your long-term health, and requires discipline and commitment, life sometimes gets in the way and tosses a few curved balls at you.

If you are feeling emotionally frazzled or 'over-cooked' you need to make a concerted effort to reverse the effects of this overload.

Some ideas that work particularly well for the empath includes:

Slow Down

Deliberately force yourself to slow down. If this means withdrawing completely, then that is what you need to do. You may simply space out social commitments a bit further apart, or schedule in some time for yourself in a busy day, or make sure that you fit in activities that will quieten your frantic mind.

Reflect

Take time to reflect on what brought you here to this point. You may feel like a long-distance runner that is out of breath with legs starting to cramp, but you need to stop, take deep breaths, and then reflect on the events leading up to this point. No recriminations, no guilt-tripping, simply look at it as objectively as possible and then tell yourself it is OK to take a break to recharge.

Learn from each event, so as to help yourself to prepare in the future to avoid the overload. Understand though that you cannot have fool-proof plans, somethings hit you harder than others, and you just need to learn to ride it out.

Heal

Allow yourself the time to heal properly before resurfacing, in whichever way works for you. You may need to scrub your kitchen or alphabetize your books, or lie on the beach for a whole day doing nothing but listen to the waves, or jump out of a plane with a parachute to feel the peace of free-floating, the number of ways to heal is as many as there are empaths.

Rediscover Nature

Most empaths find soothing and healing in nature. They need to be able to commune with the outdoors, the peace and quiet of being away from the hustle and bustle of cities and offices and busy lives.

A walk in a park, a nice long hike up in the mountains where the air is fresh, the river water cool, brownish and refreshing and the soil damp from decomposing leaves.

Or the sting of the sun and the hot wind on your cheeks out in the desert, with nothing but miles and miles of sand and xerophytes to show us how to thrive in even the harshest conditions.

Maybe thundering down the white rapids at breakneck speed or flying from tree to tree on a zip line in a rain forest. Catching a big wave on your surfboard or flying down a ski slope on your board.

Many will choose something sedate though, pottering in your garden, picking herbs for your dinner, doing quiet but long laps in a tranquil ocean or pool, playing catch with your dog in the park, or watching the sun set whilst having a picnic.

Express Your Needs

It is vitally important that you express your needs to your intimate partners and close family and friends. Explain how an overload of sensory inputs affects your mental and emotional state, what you need to do to cope and how to ground yourself.

It is important to communicate that it is about your reaction to sensory overload and that you are asking for basic accommodation and understanding. This will prevent misunderstandings and unnecessary hurt feelings.

However, it is not acceptable to expect everyone to run their lives around your emotional and sensory issues, it must be a mutually respectful accommodation, a little bit of give and take on both sides. Use your gifts to make life better for all, not to manipulate others.

Resolve Conflicts

Whilst it may sound counterintuitive, as many of our frazzled states are caused by interpersonal conflicts, in our lives, or other's, the goal should always be to resolve conflicts.

Being there for someone is more productive than being right, and sometimes conflict sprouts from silly disagreements. Agree to disagree and move on.

If someone has insulted or hurt you, the best revenge is to forgive. Forgiving someone is not for their benefit, it is for yours, as it helps you to let go.

Let go of the hurt, the anger, the pain and the residual negative emotions that overload you. It frees you from emotional obligations and wasted time and energy.

Motivate Yourself To Take Steps Against Stress

When emotional exhaustion takes over or you are in full-blown emotional burnout, motivation levels are at an extreme low, and just reading a chapter on what to do can seem like too much to ask, never mind implementing any of these strategies, and that is all right too.

So, again, slow down, sometimes you must simply stop pushing the bicycle, rebalance, and then get on it to actually cycle.

Every thousand-mile journey starts with one step, according to ancient Chinese wisdom, and as trite as it may sound from time to time, it is a universal truth.

Take one step at a time, do what you can do, small victories will help build motivation to implement more. But do whatever you can to mitigate stress, as it affects your overall health and changes your body over the long term.

Break From Technology

A large part of our busyness is related to technology, and this constant connectedness can take a heavy toll on an empath, that needs periods of connecting and periods of withdrawal.

Take a break from technology, in whichever way you need to. Close the computer for a full weekend, do not check your email after work, set your smartphone to only allow through calls from loved ones during certain hours (this can be a lifesaver during overload) and commit to technology-free family meals.

Getting lost in a Netflix binge-watching session may help you unwind to start off with, but using it constantly is not a productive coping mechanism.

Minimise Sugar And Refined Carbs

When in overload, take a break from eating or drinking anything with high sugar content or refined carbs. You may think that your energy drink is keeping you going, it is, in fact, exacerbating your overload.

Hydrate with water, with maybe some fresh lemon slices, eat lots of fruit and don't be tempted to binge on large tubs of ice cream.

Omega-3

Making healthy food choices becomes compromised during overload or stressful situations. Remember to add Omega-3 Fatty Acid rich foods to your diet, it helps reduce anxiety and long-term inflammation (54).

Examples include

- Cold water fatty fish such as salmon, herring, tuna, mackerel and sardines
- Nuts and Seeds, for instance, almonds, walnuts, pistachios, chia or flaxseeds
- Plant oils, such as flaxseed oil or soybean oil.
- Fortified foods – eggs, juice, milk and milk products are often fortified with omega-3's

Minimize caffeine, trans fats and preservatives

Make sure that you minimize foods containing trans fats and preservatives, and if caffeine makes you jittery avoid it for a while.

Some empaths may need caffeine to calm down (rare but true) but must guard against taking their caffeine in sugared drinks. Plain brewed is best.

Meditate

Meditation is a learnt process, where you train your brain to focus and to practice redirecting your thoughts. Meditation teaches us to be present in the moment.

Meditation has many benefits, including

- Increased awareness of self and surrounding
- Reduces stress
- Helps control anxiety
- Develop concentration
- Improved mood
- Self-discipline
- Increased pain-tolerance
- Improved sleep patterns
- Generate kindness

Yoga

Yoga is an ancient practice that helps us bring together body and mind by incorporating poses, breathing techniques and meditation, to reduce stress and help with relaxation.

Benefits are immediate and long-term and may include

- Increase strength, flexibility and balance
- Reduce stress, anxiety and depression
- Improve sleep and relaxation
- Improve breathing
- Fight inflammation and improve quality of life.

Incorporating yoga practice in your daily routine can help you ground yourself, feel calmer and ready to deal with whatever you are facing.

Exercise

You need to exercise at least thirty minutes a day to

stay healthy, however, this can be hard to accomplish during overload. Motivate yourself to get dressed, for exercise, then to get off the couch, out the door and before you know it you are moving and feeling better.

Some will need to engage in extreme exercise to unwind, like a long run, or a hard game of racket-ball, or hitting a punch-bag. Others will prefer swimming, gardening or going for a walk in the park.

Do whatever helps you to get rid of all that negative energy and emotions.

Healing Water

For the empath being close to or in water can be very healing. Feeling the shower spray on your back or scalp, diving into the cool depths of a crystal-clear pool, soaking in a jet tub, or braving the waves in the ocean will help relax you and soothe your soul.

The feeling of being enveloped by water, the soothing sounds, the sense of weightlessness when in the water can all contribute to helping the empath relax and releasing negative energy.

Wind In Your Hair

Sometimes the empath just needs to feel the wind in their hair, to clear the muddle of emotions and energy in their minds.

Drive with the hood down, go on motorcycle rides, horseback riding, skydiving or go walk outside in windy conditions, and feel the cobwebs blow away

Volunteer

The last thing you need when in overload is more work and more caring, but paradoxically, volunteering can help you take your mind off your own problems, and even if just for the hour it takes to serve a meal to the homeless or walk a dog at the local

SPCA. It is an excellent way to restore perspective.

Vacation

It is tempting to take a vacation when in overload, the fantasy of getting away from it all, seeing new places, experiencing new cultures and cuisines may be just the break you need.

Do consider though your propensity to sensory overload when picking a vacation spot – a quiet retreat on a small island, or game reserve, or spa may be ideal, however, a jam-packed itinerary to a tourist destination may end up being the last nail in the coffin.

Boundaries

Revisit your boundaries, make sure they make sense and examine them for breaches. Communicate them kindly but clearly to those around you to avoid future problems

Shielding

Shielding (building an imaginary bubble around yourself) may be a useful technique in the short term to cope with sensory overload and having to deal with emotional vampires, as it mentally protects you and strengthens your defense against abuse.

It is however not an appropriate long-term strategy. You may need to learn to walk away. Distance and permanent solutions are great tools for enforcing emotional freedom.

Avoid Unavailable People And Dark Triad Relationships

In order to reverse the damage and give yourself time to heal, you must avoid the unavailable people that feel so comfortable to be around, and definitely not spend time around dark triad personalities. Being around them during healing periods would be equivalent to trying to swim in the desert sands.

If You Are Struggling, Get Professional Help

Knowing yourself and your limits are crucial to not only setting a course for yourself, but also for recovery.

If you are experiencing emotional burnout or are struggling to maintain boundaries and commit to healing, get professional help.

Your general practitioner or primary care provider can refer you to an appropriate mental health care professional, to assist you in this process.

There are many volunteer organizations that provide access to professional help in you are not in a financial position to do so on your own.

Be Present

Be present today, be open to yourself, and be open to the others around you. (13) Living in the moment, letting go of what was and what could be, is the most powerful way to heal yourself.

Stop beating yourself up for what you have or have not done, stop berating yourself for only managing to do this much at this point in time.

It is what it is. This moment is enough.

Evolving

What lies behind us and

what lies before us are tiny matters compared to what lies within us.

Oliver Wendell Holmes

Evolving As An Empath

Being labeled as 'too sensitive for your own good' or mocked for needing alone time can intimidate some of the most aware amongst human beings. Understanding how heightened sensitivities are determined by many factors such as genetics, environment, early life connections, nurturing and adverse events can help the empath to self-acceptance and to build a happy, healthy and thriving life.

All individuals need to feel safe, accepted, loved and respected, no matter their physical appearance, social status or accomplishments.

For the empath to evolve, they need to embrace their connection with emotions and energy, their ability to sense what other people cannot, protect themselves from known triggers and predators, and strengthen their belief in their own abilities and significance.

Evolving comes from the Latin word 'evolver' (to unroll) and it means to 'develop gradually', or to change over time. Evolving as a person includes constant growth to reach your full potential as a human being with an emphasis on self-realization.

It is not a one-step process or a short-term project to plan and execute, it is a way of life, constantly evolving into a better version of yourself. This may sound counterintuitive to living in the moment, however, being present means accepting what is and appreciating it, whilst striving to grow in whatever direction is needed.

'You cannot go on indefinitely being just an ordinary, decent egg. You must be hatched, or go bad'
C.S. Lewis

For the empath to evolve, they need to

- Embrace their gifts, and understand that it is not a burden but a wonderful contribution to make the world a kinder place for all
- Find self-acceptance, and develop a strong core of identity, underscored by resilience, hope and optimism
- Share their empathic gifts in their relationships, be that at home, with friends, at work, when meeting strangers in need of help
- Practice self-care, diligently and with love, to strengthen and protect themselves
- Be authentic and direct
- Have integrity
- Practice self-compassion
- Adhere to boundaries
- Allow themselves the time to recharge.

- Accept their own idiosyncrasies and work on their weaknesses
- Practice gratitude
- Grow outside their comfort zone
- Learn how to thrive

But how do you move outside your comfort zones to grow as a person so you can lead a full, rich life?

Grow Outside Your Comfort Zone

Continuous growth takes a dogged determination and tenacity, it is not about the grand gestures, such as extreme fitness programmes or visiting a diet farm, but making small changes every day to move towards a healthy, fulfilling life.

It may be something as simple as drinking an extra cup of water or saying no to one request, but eventually, it will build up into a habit and then become second nature.

Small victories empower and reengergise anyone struggling to move forward. Slay the dragons that are holding you back one tiny change at a time.

What a man can be, he must be.
This need we call self-actualisation.
Abraham Maslow

Maslow believed that all people have an inborn need for self-actualization that is the need to be all they can be. He postulated that in order to achieve these goals, one had to fulfill 'lower order' needs first, such as food, safety, love, and self-esteem.

These five needs have stood the test of time, even though many believe them not be met in hierarchical order, but to be present at all times.

Thus, self-actualizing individuals are:
- Concerned with personal growth

- Self-aware
- Less concerned with other's opinions
- Trying to fulfill their potential

Personal Effectiveness

Personal effectiveness includes using all the resources at your disposal (energy, time, talents, etc.) in all spheres of life (personal, work) to achieve your goals and master your life.

Increasing personal effectiveness involves:

- Identifying what you really want from life, what are the things that bring you true satisfaction and a sense of fulfillment and happiness
- Identifying your values and beliefs – values are deep-rooted beliefs that guide your everyday thinking and actions. They give you a clearer sense of self, helps you focus and thus provides energy to do the things that really matter and become more effective. Making sure you honor

your own beliefs, and not those of friends or what you think is expected of you helps you build authenticity. Pretending to be someone other than who you really are is exhausting and you are most likely going to be found out as a fraud or a wimp whom just follows the today crowd.
- Allowing yourself to follow your dreams is the ultimate gift you can give yourself, doing what really makes you happy and content.
- Eliminating distorted thinking can be a tall order, and sometimes you need to seek professional help with a counsellor or coach, to help you eliminate your distorted thinking about who you are, how you think, believe and act, by reflecting it back to you, so you can observe your distorted thinking objectively and find your real truth.
- Setting goals and working to achieve them – if you do not set goals you cannot stretch yourself to grow and become more effective, you will meander along disparate roads and plod

through life wondering what happened. Set attainable goals, don't build castles in the sky, and work at achieving them, always stretching a bit further.

- Prioritizing the most important things in life, in your life, is a key step to evolving. Follow the things that matter, spend your precious time and effort on your priorities. Eliminate clutter and emotional baggage and let go of ideas, things and people that do not contribute to making your life better.
- Developing self-confidence, creativity, persistence and problem-solving skills – spending time improving your cognitive and emotional skills every day is an investment in the future. Read as much as you can, broaden your mind, play mind-building games and have challenging and deep conversations with family and friends. Enroll for a course in something you love, or volunteer to teach others.
- Streamlining your inner and outer images – to live an authentic life you cannot pretend to be one

person and actually be another, or as some people are wont to do, be different people for different people based on what they think is expected. It is exhausting, dishonest, stressful and disastrous for your mental health. Accept yourself for who you are, and live an authentic life

- Getting organized can sound incredibly mundane and boring, but some basic organization can bring stability and peace to your life. Clear out clutter (nothing worse for making you feel crowded), find a place for everything, roughly plan your time according to priorities set, and allow for mishaps and emergencies and makes sure everyone does their fair share.
- Getting feedback as often as possible, in order to reflect and reevaluate where we are on our journey can be very useful. We are not aware of what we don't know, and if we open up to constructive feedback we may discover new ways of doing things or new strengths to develop.

Ideas To Help You Evolve As An Empath

- Open yourself up to learning as much as possible – stretch yourself
- Be willing to feel awkward or uncomfortable when you try something new
- Stretch your mind by reading a lot to understand world events, how people think and behave.
- Question your own thinking and behaviour patterns, understanding why you do things will help you to work on strengths and eliminate weaknesses
- Learn from people that know more
- Share your thought processes with your closest allies
- Ask for help if you are struggling
- Go out and meet new people
- Learn to walk away from negativity
- Try to understand why things are done in a certain way
- Travel if you can

- Try new things, no matter how scary or ridiculous they may be, for example
- Go ski-diving
- Watch a soap opera (if you have never done that before)
- Talk to someone you would not normally approach at a function
- Eat at a different restaurant
- Read a comic book
- Learn about different religions
- Go skinny-dipping at night
- Learn to steer clear of instant gratification, work on the long game
- Get up and try again if you fail at something or revert to old habits
- Develop persistence – keep at growing slowly, quietly, persistently.
- Integrate new habits into the fabric of your life.
- Remember, the magic happens outside your comfort zone

Image from quotefancy.com

Conclusion

Being an empath is about accepting your gifts of expanded sensitivity, living your best life and using your talents to help others understand their emotions so they can heal.

However, it is not easy living with so much emotion and energy, and often being overwhelmed due to bucket loads of jarring sensory inputs. Holding on to negativity, anger, frustration, pain, and sadness on behalf of another can be debilitating.

The empath owes it to themselves, and their loved ones, to get a clear understanding of their gifts, talents and needs, and to learn to communicate these.

As not all empaths are the same, their level of empathy may vary, their expression of their gifts may assist or bewilder others and their periods of withdrawal may debilitate relationships, friendships and make loved ones seriously question their sanity. Emotional lability is a constant companion and not always invited or wanted.

Having looked at the reasons for empaths feeling so much, the origins of these abilities and the downfalls of being an empath, it is clear that a deeper understanding is required, from both the empath and their communities.

Using the four R's to modulate their swings – reevaluate, recognize, resilience, and reverse – the empath can build a strong resistance to the pitfalls of being too open and available and avoid the nightmarish symbiotic pairing up with emotional vampires and the dark triad personalities.

By applying themselves diligently to small daily steps they can evolve and thrive by living healthy happy lives.

References

1. Dissociation of Cognitive and Emotional Empathy: The Multifaceted Empathy Test for Children and Adolescents: MET-J. al, L. Poustka et. 2010.

2. Bérangère Thirioux, François Birault and Nematollah Jaafari. Empathy Is a Protective Factor of Burnout in Physicians: New Neuro-Phenomenological Hypotheses Regarding Empathy and Sympathy in Care Relationship.

3. Zahavi, D. Simulation, projection, and empathy. . 2008, S. 514–522.

4. Damasio, A., and Carvalho, G. B. The nature of feelings: evolutionary and neurobiological origins. Nat. Rev. Neurosci. 2013, Bd. 14, S. 143–152.

5. Blanke, O. Multisensory brain mechanisms of bodily self-consciousness. . Nat. Rev. Neurosci. 13, 2012, S. 556–571.

6. Thirioux, B. Perception et apperception dans l'empathie: une critique des neurons miroir, in Les Paradoxes de l'Empathie. [Hrsg.] and A. Cuckiers eds

P. Attigui. Paris: CNRS Editions. 2011, S. 73–94.

7.The cognitive and neural time course of empathy and sympathy: an electrical neuroimaging study on self-other interaction. Thirioux, B., Mercier, M. R., Blanke, O., and Berthoz, A. 2014, Neuroscience , S. 286–306.

8.Goleman, Daniel. Empathy.

9.William A. Gentry, Todd J. Weber, and Golnaz Sadri. White Paper: Empathy in the Workplace. A Tool for Effective Leadership. s.l. : Center for Creative Leadership.

10.The Empathy Effect. Helen Riess, MD.

11.Interventions to cultivate physician empathy: a. al, Kelm et. 2014, BMC Medical Education, Bd. 14, S. 219.

12.Therapeutic empathy: what it is and what it isn't. al, Howick J. et. 2018, Journal of the Royal Society of Medicine, Bd. 111(7), S. 233-236.

13.What Does Empathy Contribute in This Age of Science and Technology? Suzanne M. Olbricht, MD.

2, August 2015, Cutis, Bd. 96, S. 78-79.

14. Weiner, Irving B. und Craighead, W. Edward. The Corsini Encyclopedia of Psychology. s.l. : John Wiley & Sons., 2010. S. 810. ISBN 978-0-470-17026-7..

15. Goleman, Daniel. Focus. The Hidden Driver of Excellence. 2013.

16. The Tao of Doing Good. Navigating between anger and acceptance in solving social issues. Allyn, David. s.l. : Stanford Social Innovation Review, 2012.

17. Who Cares? Revisiting Empathy in Asperger Syndrome. Rogers K, Dziobek I, Hassenstab J, Wolf OT, Convit A. 2007, J Autism Dev Disord, S. 709-715.

18. Neurogenetic variations in norepinephrine availability enhance perceptual vividness. Todd, Rebecca M. und al., et. 2015, Journal of Neuroscience.

19. Epistasis between 5-HTTLPR and ADRA2B polymorphisms influences attentional bias for emotional information in healthy volunteers. Naudts, Kris H., et al. 2012, International Journal of Neurospycholpharmacology.

20. Hatfield, E., Cacioppo, J. T. and Rapson, R. L. Emotional contagion. . Cambridge: : Cambridge University Press., 1994.

21. NIH.

22. Lacobani, M. Mirroring people: the science of empathy and how we connect with others. . New York: : Farrar, Straus, and Giroux., 2008.

23. Journal of Neuroscience.

24. The Science Behind Empathy and Empaths. MD, Judith Orloff. 2017, Psychology Today.

25. Super Empaths are Real.

26. Empathy hurts: Compassion for another increases both sensory and affective components of pain perception . Marco Loggia (Harvard) Jeffrey S Mogil, Mary Catherine Bushnell (NIH).

27. The fear factor: how one emotion connects altruists, psychopaths & everyone in between. . Marsh, A. New York: : Basic Books., 2017.

28. New-research-may-support-the-existence-of-empaths.

29. Dissociation of Cognitive and Emotional Empathy: The Multifaceted Empathy Test for Children and Adolescents.

30. Effect_of_visual_stimuli_of_pain_on_empathy_brain_network_in_people_with_and_without_Autism_Spectrum_Disorder.

31. Five-Factor Model of Personality. Christopher J. Soto, Joshua J. Jackson. 2018, OxfordBibliographies.

32. Measuring Individual Differences in Empathy: Evidence for a Multidimensional Approach. Davis, Mark H. 1, 1983, Journal of Personality and Social Psychology., Bd. 44, S. 113–26. .

33. The Empath's Survival Guide. Orloff, Dr. Judith.

34. The "false consensus effect": An egocentric bias in social perception and attribution processes. Lee Ross, David Greene, Pamela House. 1977, Semantic Scholar.

35. Does_Feeling_Empathy_Lead_to_Compassion_Fatigue_or_Compassion_Satisfaction_The_Role_of_Time_Perspective.

36. Neural Responses to Ingroup and Outgroup

Members' Suffering Predict Individual Differences in Costly Helping".. Hein, Grit, et al. 1, 2010, Neuron, Bd. 68, S. 149–160.

37. Emotional Vampires: People who Drain you Dry. PhD, Albert Bernstein. 2012.

38. The Six Pillars of Self-esteem: the definitive work on self-esteem by the leading pioneer in the field. Branden, Nathaniel. 1995.

39. The Subtle Art of not Giving a F*ck. Manson, Mark.

40. Maslach Burnout Inventory Manual. ResearchGate.

41. Empathy at the Heart of Darkness: Empathy deficits that bind the dark triad and those that mediate indirect relational aggression. Heym, Nadja et al. 2019, Frontiers in Psychiatry.

42. Jones, D. N., Paulhus, D. L. Differentiating the dark triad within the interpersonal circumplex. [Hrsg.] L. M. Horowitz und S. N. Strack. Handbook of interpersonal theory and research. New York: Guilford, 2010, S. 249-67.

43. An Examination of the Dark Triad Constructs with Regard to Prosocial Behavior. Tackett, Jack A Palmer and Seth. 5, 2018, Acta Psychopathologica, Bd. 4.

44. Do I win, does the company win, or do we both win? Moderate traits of the Dark Triad and profit maximization. Marcia Figueredo D'Souza, et al. 4, 2019, Revista Contabilidade & Finanças, Bd. 79.

45. Sensory Processing Sensitivity: A review in the light of the evolution of biological responsivity. Elaine N. Aron, Arthur Aron and Jadzia Jagiellowicz. X, 2012, Personality and Social Psychology Review, Bd. XX, S. 1-21.

46. Sensory Processing Sensitivity in the Context of Environmental Sensitivity: A Critical Review and Development of Research Agenda. al, Corina U. Grven et. 2018, Preprints 2018.

47. The Highly Sensitive Person: How to Thrive when the World Overwhelms You. Elaine N. Arn, Ph.D.

48. Differential susceptibility to the environment: An evolutionary -neurodevelopment theory. al, Bruce J. Ellis et. 2011, Development and Psychopathology, Bd.

23, S. 7-28.

49. Social Anxiety Disorder: more then just shyness. NIH: National Institute of Mental Health.

50. Bipolar Disorder. NIH: National Institute of Mental Health.

51. The balance between feeling and knowing: affective and cognitive empathy are reflected in the brain's intrinsic functional dynamics. al, Cox CL et. 6, 2012, Soc Cogn Affect Neurosci, Bd. 7, S. 727-37.

52. Borderline Personality Disorder. NIH: National Institute of Mental Health.

53. Leadership Vitality. Ehlers, W.

54. Resilience. Psychology Today.

55. Food for Mood: Relevance of Nutritional Omega-3 Fatty Acids for Depression and Anxiety. Laye, Thomas Larrieu and Sophie. 2018, Frontiers in Psychology, Bd. 9, S. 1047.

56. I know how you feel: the warm-altruistic personality profile and the empathic brain. Haas, BW, et al. 3, 2015, PLOS ONE., Bd. 10, S. e0120639.

Disclaimer

The information contained in this book and its components, is meant to serve as a comprehensive collection of strategies that the author of this book has done research about. Summaries, strategies, tips and tricks are only recommendations by the author, and reading this book will not guarantee that one's results will exactly mirror the author's results.

The author of this book has made all reasonable efforts to provide current and accurate information for the readers of this book. The author and its associates will not be held liable for any unintentional errors or omissions that may be found.

The material in the book may include information by third parties. Third party materials comprise of opinions expressed by their owners. As such, the author of this book does not assume responsibility or liability for any third party material or opinions.

The publication of third party material does not constitute the author's guarantee of any information, products, services, or opinions contained within third party material. Use of third party material does not guarantee that your results will mirror our results. Publication of such third party material is simply a recommendation and expression of the author's own opinion of that material.

Whether because of the progression of the Internet, or the unforeseen changes in company policy and editorial submission guidelines, what is stated as fact at the time of this writing may become outdated or inapplicable later.

This book is copyright ©2019 by **Joseph Salinas** with all rights reserved. It is illegal to redistribute, copy, or create derivative works from this book whole or in parts. No parts of this report may be reproduced or retransmitted in any forms whatsoever without the written expressed and signed permission from the author.

Made in the USA
Columbia, SC
03 June 2020